CRACK THE ESSAY

Secrets of Argumentative Writing

Revealed

By Simon Black

ISBN-10: 0999678299
ISBN: 13: 978-0999678299

FIRST EDITION 2018

Published by Gramercy House Publishing

www.cracktheessay.com

Dedicated to my mother, who stayed up late with me one night long ago when I was in high school to help me write my first really good paper, an analysis of "Elegy Written in a Country Churchyard". You taught me to love literature and writing, Mom, so that I saw the essay not as a burdensome task, but as a possibility for the unveiling of insight and joy.

INTRODUCTION

Are you stuck on an essay? Are you unable to translate the great ideas in your head to the written page? Do you feel like you are way smarter than you sound on paper? Maybe you're frustrated. Maybe you've decided you're "not a good writer." Maybe your teachers even told you this. Maybe you've convinced yourself that when it comes to college writing, you just can't do it well. Guess what! You're wrong. You can write like a masterful sage, a brilliant rhetorician – a great scholar. I'm going to show you exactly how to do it. It's not a complicated mish mosh of hard to understand principles. Academic writing can be an exciting adventure that anybody can master. It doesn't have to be a chore.

There are two types of writing – 1) "bad" writing – dull, procedural, dutiful going through the motions type of writing. Or 2) "good" writing – writing that creates a world, a universe, a big bang; in other words, creative writing. You know almost immediately when you begin reading which type of writing you are encountering. By the end of the first paragraph it's completely clear. The author either has it, or the author doesn't.

For years I thought people were either born writers or they weren't. Even after years of teaching writing I was in my heart slightly skeptical about my ability to turn a "bad" writer into a "good" one.

My breakthrough came when it dawned on me that students were starting the writing process from a place of defeat. They were treating their essays like an assortment of words on paper – a rather labored, phony, meaningless, paint-by numbers drivel. They weren't treating their papers like works of art. They weren't seeing the creative possibility of the form itself – academic writing. The students weren't seeing their papers as worlds unto themselves.

That's what a great text is, after all – a textual cosmos, a universe that was made by a God-like power, the author, through an act of creative will.

When I began presenting the writing process this way, I had a lot more success. The system I developed I called "Cosmological Writing."

We all know the creation story of the Bible – And God said, "Let there be Light." God spoke, and the cosmos was created by the power of his speaking. There are many stories in mythology about how various versions of God created the cosmos out of nothing – *ex nihilo*. These creation myths portray God as the ultimate craftsman. For instance, in the Egyptian myth Ptah is a God who was such a master of his craft that he could create things simply by naming them. The simple act speaking materialized the things of the world into existence.

The writer is often compared to God. After all, we speak of the "omniscient narrator," since the author all knowing about the world of his text. The writing voice of the student, however, rarely succeeds in achieving this sort of authorial power. Student papers rarely have the appearance of sacred, or even interesting or artistic texts.

Until I began teaching the cosmological method, I never saw true authorial power in my classroom. This potential power of the student writer had been suppressed by years of toiling under the oppression of the "five paragraph essay" in high school, by the horrifying experience of writing "the personal essay" on a college application, or by the mind-numbing experience of most freshman comp classes.

By the time they got to me, though, the students were not completely dead. I discovered through application of these methods that the powerful authorial voice of the downtrodden student could be brought to life. Students began to see their essays as worlds, as universes, as creations, rather than chores assigned to them by taskmasters.

Cosmological writing creates a place that is inhabited by a living, breathing force of argument. Even though it's just an essay, students can learn to create this place through these simple tools and exercises that I provide. Almost immediately, though, and even before they have had time to digest many of the tools and techniques, their writing improves because they come at the text with a creative attitude, one of possibility and art. Teachers and students alike will see immediate results.

I found that almost anybody can write like a God if given the correct instructions and the right tools. You can do it, too. Luckily, you have stumbled across the keys to the academic kingdom. Now nothing can stop you from writing like the highest-level scholars at your institution. However, be warned, although I reveal the tricks of the trade, it will still take effort and perseverance to master them. Rather than tricks, after all, these tools are merely forms with which you can frame your thoughts, your ideas and your originality. Rather than a system of fill in the blanks, what I offer here is a tool box for you to build your rhetorical dream home, along with a different way of looking at the art of academic prose. Once you master it, you will indeed have discovered your own true, unique scholarly super power. You will have cracked the essay.

NOTE: How to Use this Book

Teachers, I recommend going through three chapters a week as you develop a writing project with your students. That means your students will have several weeks to finish a draft of their essay before Chapter 11 when my approach re-writing is presented. Then, another two weeks can be spent on the rewriting chapter as they revise their essay. For your next writing assignment, go back to the beginning and review the chapters at a more rapid pace as the students will be much more conversant with the terminology and process involved.

Students: The book will take you through the stages of making your first draft of an essay. Thus, if you already have an assignment from one of your teachers, you can use the first chapters to address this assignment. Then, Chapters 12-16 walk you through the re-writing process.

If you are using this book on your own, you can find writing assignments and much other information on the web site: www.cracktheessay.com. Go to the web site to find these resources. If you enter your email you will be sent an additional tool for your writing process – a compendium of additional tricks of the trade that will greatly improve the scholarly tone of your work.

Chapter One

The Cosmological Difference

Why shouldn't an argumentative essay be considered aesthetically beautiful? I know it's not a poem or a painting or a symphony. Nevertheless, the essay contains formal characteristics that can be as pleasing to the soul as Beethoven's *Fifth*. These characteristics are primarily distinctions – insights about the way things relate to one another in the real world and in the higher realm of ideas. To create these distinctions takes creativity, intelligence and artistic sensibility. In other words, cosmological writing isn't easy – but with my method it can be achieved by anybody.

Once you are on this road, this "heavy metal" way of writing instead of limping along with your pen, you are never going to go back to the old ways. It is very exciting to create a vibrant world with your words. Students report the feeling of satisfaction when they are done with their drafts that, as though they have "made" something.

What are we making?

A beautiful structure that contains interesting and enlightening moments – that is what we are aiming for.

You must pick up your artist's palette and put on your beret. When you sit down at your computer, you are not doing something laborious and perfunctory. You are going to build something. You're not even sure yet what it is, but if you follow the steps of this book, when you are done you will have it – this beautiful structure with interesting and enlightening moments. You will be very proud of your pages when you pick them up out of your printer. When you look at them, you'll know they are really something. They are not just pages. They are a little bit of your soul that you have managed to put out there into the world. They are a little bit of your wisdom and your complexity. They are a little bit of the magical essence that is you.

What I'm trying to inculcate here at the beginning is an attitude of engagement.

Engagement

If you asked me what is the primary difference between student writing and professional writing, I would tell you that it is the level of engagement with the material that a professional scholar exhibits. What is engagement? It seems like a hard to pin down concept, some nebulous sense of "depth" or "enthusiasm." Some writers seem to really care about what they are saying, while students often seem to be just going thought the motions. Why?

They *are* just going through the motions. Most student writing has the diffident voice and the unconfident tone of the underling. It exhibits the symptoms of profoundly low self-esteem, low affect, and perhaps dissociation from reality. If we were to diagnose our students based on their essays, I think most of them would be put on a heavy course of anti-depressants.

It occurred to me one day in the classroom that it was my fault as much as the students'. I was the sage on the stage, the POWER, the king of my class room. And they were my subjects. No wonder they sounded so weak in their writing. They *were* weak.

I decided to give the students back their power. I told them I didn't want them to respond to my writing prompts like mediocre underlings. I wanted them to express themselves through my prompt in a powerful way, a new "heavy metal" method of writing.

One of the first problems I identified was the notion of a "prompt" itself—a writing topic that is given, prescribed and mandated by a powerful professor. It immediately situates the student as an underling, a peon. No wonder students feel inhibited, tongue-tied and shy about their ideas. From the get-go they are the hamstrung by the idea of subordination to the prompt. The prompt is the "law". It was delivered to the student by the King or at least God's messenger – the professor.

Your professor is not King or Queen.

The author is the power. In every piece of prose, fiction or non-fiction, the authorial voice is the power behind all creation therein. Sometimes the voice is omniscient, sometimes humbler. But in all cases, the author's desk is where the buck stops--not the professor's or anyone else's. The professor can give you a grade, but he or she cannot give you – engagement.

CLAIM THE PROMPT like the God that you are! Write your own prompt inside the professor's prompt. In other words, stake your claim to the writing topic within the guidelines given. You do this by first writing about what you think really matters.

ENGAGEMENT KEY NUMBER ONE

Raise the stakes.

In Hollywood movies, the bigger the budget, the bigger the stakes –thus many tentpole movies have at the center of their tension the highest stakes possible – the destruction of the world. If the hero doesn't succeed the world will end.

Now in essay writing the stakes don't need to be quite that high. Nevertheless, we want to make the stakes as high as possible, even if it means exaggeration.

Exaggeration is not a sin in writing – it is an acceptable method of raising the stakes, which is referred to rhetorically as hyperbole.

To be slightly hyperbolic about the issue you're arguing is to signal to the audience that it should wake up and pay attention because the consequences of this matter might be bigger than expected.

Regarding the prompt of marijuana legislation, for instance, it is possible to emphasize the seriousness of the issue in several ways. One might be the public safety issues involved. Might driving while stoned lead to increase in traffic fatalities? That is a general way of appealing to the audience. But why not make it personal? What if your child were killed by a stoned driver after legalization? Would you support the legalization of marijuana? Of course not.

Another way to raise the stakes might be to appeal to the theme of injustice, again, keeping it personal. What if the life of someone you love were ruined by a marijuana conviction? He/she can no longer become a lawyer, a policeman or even serve in the army. He/she may lose the job they already have, or he/she may serve time in prison. And why? Because he/she inhaled smoke from a naturally occurring weed.

In order to raise the stakes, writers appeal to emotion, pain, need, value, urgency, ethics, self-preservation, crisis avoidance and more. But even the most dry and unemotional appeal – logic – can be heightened. The key is to believe that it matters to yourself first. If you can't convince yourself of the importance and urgency of the main tension, then you haven't found the right main tension. Search for another one that you can respond to with more urgency.

ENGAGEMENT KEY NUMBER TWO

There is more at stake in the universal than the local.

There might be something at stake in the specific instance you are writing about – for instance, the application of affirmative action at Harvard University. But there is always more at stake in the general principle that underlies the specific application of that principle. In other words, there is more at stake in the nationwide application of affirmative action principles. That is because many more students will be affected, not just students at Harvard.

In the case of removal of a Confederate monument in Charlottesville, Virginia, there is a lot at stake. Protestors might appear, and counter-protesters might meet them. Violence might erupt. Thousands of locals might have a stake in the outcome. But think about the issue of historical monuments in general. There are historical monuments in every town and every city in the country. If we are going to start evaluating which ones need to be brought down, that is an issue that in general might affect millions and millions of people across the country and then billions across the globe. The idea of judging the past based on the standards of the present is hugely polarizing. Some want to wipe the slate clean while others want to preserve the heroes of the past.

This is what is known as looking to the universal question underneath the specific. There in the universal you will find a fundamental tension. Tension serves to keep your reader interest. Tension in academic writing comes from dialectic opposition of forces.

ENGAGEMENT KEY NUMBER THREE

Find a Basic Dialectic in the Writing Prompt

A dialectic is two opposing forces. It can be found at the heart of the basic question beneath the writing prompt.

Let's say the writing prompt is: should marijuana be legalized in your state? This may or may not interest you. But there is a universal question beneath the question that has nothing to do with marijuana per se. This is where you must look to find "universal engagement." Universal engagement is the term I use here for engaging the largest amount of readers for the largest amount of time. Marijuana as a topic is only likely to engage a percentage of your readers. But there is a larger question that will engage the universe.

How do you find the deeper question beneath the question? While it seems like the topic is "marijuana", the second word of the sentence, the topic that can engage the mind at a deeper level is found at the other end of the sentence—"the state." How far should the government go in regulating personal behavior? That is the interesting question, one that all minds can get interested in. The role we have assigned government under the social contract is constantly being revised by history. At this moment in time the revision is including the government's regulation of drugs, but also the government's regulation of sexual orientation, immigration status and a few other hot button issues. What all the hot button issues have in common is the philosophical question of how far should a government impinge upon individuals?

WHITHER THE DIALECTIC?

Each writing prompt you receive will at some point boil down to a dialectic, a binary pair of choices, an opposition of two forces. In this case of marijuana legalization, it is the individual versus the collective. The interests of one person who wants to buy marijuana are up against the interests of the group, who have previously ordained that marijuana is forbidden.

How does this dialectic help us get engaged in the topic? Well, we all live under some form of government. We all attempt to forge an individual life within the context of a collective whole. There is a tension that we feel at every moment, perhaps unconsciously. No matter who we are, we can relate to this dialectic, because it is inscribed in our daily activities. We make the decision not to cross the street because the light has not changed to red yet, and the group prescribes that we wait for the walk sign. However, we also know that jaywalking, freelancing, disobeying is possible. If there is no traffic, maybe these laws don't apply to us. Maybe we don't agree with this traffic law at all. But we make a calculation. How much will this cost us if we go against the collective? Fines, personal injuries, etc. These possible consequences are presented to our unconscious mind in a flash. And this is just our first stop in our day.

It is at this level that we can write about the pedestrian topic of marijuana legalization with depth, urgency and relevance. Like a scholar.

"The interesting question the marijuana legalization debate brings up is how far should our government go in limiting or delimiting our personal, private, consumption behavior?"

But read Key Number One again. Notice the Key is not find the dialectic. It states find *a* dialectic. Are there other dialectics? Yes. There are many. For instance, another dialectic beneath the idea of marijuana legalization is pleasure versus responsibility. Do we live life for the simple pleasure and endorphin rush (marijuana) or is there a greater calling than the pleasing sensations in the brain that a drug can provide? Are we called to serve some less endorphin-releasing discipline? (WORK?)

The dialectic statement here would read, "The real question is why are we here – to feel sensations of great pleasure in our brains or to accomplish something with the moments of our day? The debate on marijuana legalization may seem like it's about law enforcement but it's really about the meaning of our time here on earth."

Here are some other common dialectics underlying 99% of all possible writing prompts and essay topics.

Nature versus Nurture

Is the behavior a result of something inborn that is essential or innate to humans, or is it a result of something learned, conditioned and "nurtured" by society and culture. For instance, if you are writing about anything to do with crime, rehabilitation, security, inequality, and yes, even marijuana, this dialectic could apply.

Dialectic statement:

"Some people are for marijuana legalization and some are against. But the striking thing is that this division of opinion has much more to do with the way in which the person being polled was brought up, educated, and cultured. You are far more likely to be against marijuana legalization, for instance, if you were brought up in a strict religious household. Conservative, evangelicals, religious folk tend to believe that we are born in a world of temptation that must be resisted. Marijuana is one of those temptations. Strong resistance to these evil forces will be rewarded in the afterlife. However, liberals tend to see the individual as inherently good. In the liberal view, resisting temptation isn't the challenge of life. Making a better world here on earth is the goal. Perhaps marijuana makes life better here for some folks."

Capitalism versus Socialism

Is it better to let the free market determine things or to regulate it with some more intrusive policing government authority?

Dialectic statement:

"If there is a demand for a product, capitalism says that it is our duty to supply that demand. If it is not harming anybody, any attempts at prohibiting the marketing of a certain product are anti-capitalist."

Moderation versus Abstinence

Is it better to avoid something dangerous or addictive entirely (sex, alcohol, video games) through a complete prohibition of this indulgence or is best to allow moderate consumption and responsible indulgence?

Dialectic statement:

"With regard to marijuana, prohibition seems not to have worked. It's been illegal forever but still it's everywhere."

The natural world versus the civilized world

Yes, it's true that marijuana grows naturally. But so does poison. Don't we try to avoid poison ivy? Should we try to avoid this poison weed?

And there are many more underlying dialectics. These might include:

Cash vs. Health,
Urban vs. Country,
Colonist vs. Colony,
Powerful vs. Powerless,
Globalization vs. Local Identity
White vs. Non-White
Majority vs. Minority
Freedom vs. License
Reason vs. Emotion
Intellect vs. Soul
Reality vs. Illusion
The Real World vs. Fantasy
Essential and Innate vs. Socially Constructed
Real vs. Artificial
Choice vs. Determinism
Fate vs. Will
Work vs. Play
Art vs. Entertainment
Rich vs. Poor

Healthy vs. Sick
Old vs. Young
East vs. West
First World vs. Third World

Exercise:

Choose a dialectic from above or find an entirely new binary opposition or tension and apply it to the following seemingly superficial writing prompt. Write a paragraph explaining how this dialectic lies underneath, how it is the real question beneath the less "real" question on the surface.

Prompt 1:

How has technology changed the way people communicate? Has it improved or hurt it?

Underlying dialectic:

_____ vs. _____

Explain:

_____

_____

_____

_____

Prompt 2:

How has your neighborhood shaped you and made you into the person you are today?

_____ vs. _____

Explain:

_____

_____

_____

_____

Prompt 3:

Nudity in public art – yes or no?

_____ vs. _____

Explain:

_____

_____

Hints for finding the underlying dialectic

Look at the other end of the sentence. There are usually two elements in the prompt that can be seen at odds with each other. For the examples above:

1. Good communication vs. bad communication
2. Neighborhood/person
3. Art/public

An essay would then go on to define what is good what is bad, what is a neighborhood, what is art, what is public? See Chapter Two, "Defining Your Terms."

ENGAGEMENT KEY NUMBER 4

Stake out a mediative position between the two extremes of the dialectic.

Students often don't understand that they can have a strong thesis that admits validity to both sides of the argument. This is called a mediative position. If two parties are in a conflict they rely on a judge or an outside mediator to arbitrate their case. Similarly, academic writers are rhetorical arbitrators who normally mediate their audience to a position of some centrality.

For instance, the position you defend in marijuana legalization might be a mediative one between outright prohibition of marijuana and complete deregulation of the marijuana market. For instance, a student might argue for legalization of all but the edible candy marijuana. Or the student might argue for local coding and zoning laws to delimit the sale of the drug.

In a writing prompt about affirmative action, the mediative position might not be a complete banning of considering race in college admissions. A student might argue that some consideration of racial and ethnic balance in a university population should be permitted. This position does not go as far as affirmative action in the purest sense, but it does go somewhere.

The center is not a place of no action, it is just a place of considered and careful action. Critical thinkers often arrive at the most considered and careful position. Only non-critical thinkers sway to the impulsive, extreme or cognitively distorted position.

Staking out this center between two extremes, what Aristotle referred to as the golden mean, might involve opposing argument, concession, or qualification of your own thesis. We deal with this in Chapter Eight. But for now, it is enough to know that what we are engaging in is ultimately not propagandistic advocacy but critical, mediative thinking. To mediate effectively you must remain enthusiastically engaged in the dialectical tension that exists underneath your writing prompt.

REVIEW: Engagement Keys 1-4

1. Raise the stakes
2. Look to the universal question.
3. Find the dialectic
4. Create a mediation between the two extremes

Let's go through the following prompt and work this four-step process.

Prompt: The prevalence of sexual assault on campus has led some to argue for an end to Greek life, as fraternities are often the center of the partying scene, and the locale of sexual misunderstanding and/or assault. Should fraternities be allowed to continue campus?

1. Raise the stakes: imagine your daughter is going off to school where supposedly one in five girls are raped. How do you feel?
2. Look to the universal question: (go beyond the local – the fraternity, to the more global – the university or the culture at large) How can we create a culture where women don't feel threatened?
3. Find the dialectic – there is a tension between the need to protect females and the danger of villainizing innocent males.
4. Form a mediative position. Perhaps we can have fraternities but educate students so that the party scene self-regulates regarding overdrinking and sexually inappropriate behaviors?

Prompt: Is it all fake news in the main stream media?

1. Raise the stakes: we rely on news to show us the world. If they've been lying to us all this time, then we've been living inside a delusional matrix. How do we get out?

2. Look to the universal question: (go beyond the local). Going beyond the news, it is apparent that language can manipulate truth, in any context. How do we ensure that language in general is used to communicate and not delude us?

3. Find the dialectic – communication vs. manipulation.

4. Mark out a mediative position: The news watcher can use critical thinking to question the "facts" that are being delivered to him. We might never be able to legislate that people use language truthfully rather than manipulatively, but we as listeners can learn to discern, and thus the more truthful speakers will be the more successful.

Now You Try

Now try by yourself. Use the four keys to develop an engaged approach the following prompt:

Prompt: Do young adults like dystopian fiction because their world is dystopian or is it a mistaken interpretation of their world that attracts them to horrific sci-fi futures like the Hunger Games?

1. Raise the stakes (how can we engage with this topic as though it really mattered?)

_____

_____

_____

_____

_____

_____

_____

_____

_____

_____

_____

2. Go beyond the local (beyond young adult dystopian fiction, why is the negative more attractive than the positive in fictional worlds?)

_____

_____

_____

_____

_____

3. Find the dialectic: (hint: look toward the middle of the sentence)

_____

_____

_____

_____

4. Form a mediative position: (hint: between the two extremes)

_____

_____

_____

_____

_____

_____

Chapter Two

DEFINE YOUR TERMS ON YOUR TERMS–NOT THEIRS

After you have staked out the thesis and the dialectic underneath the thesis, the next task in rhetoric is to define exactly what you're talking about. Rather than a dictionary definition, what you are going to offer the reader is an original definition that only you, great scholar, has thought of. Remember, scholarship is not about humility. It is about intellectual ego. You must present to your audience as "the one who knows." How do you do this? Again, by playing God. By making your own definition for things you are engaging in the generative act of creation. You are becoming what I call "cosmological". You have created an eco-system, a universe, that the reader can only find under your auspices, under your authorial voice. All great authors are like this. If you want to read something Faulknerian you don't read Proust, you read Faulkner.

Most cosmological myth stories begin with a big bang of some sort. You, too, scholar, will begin with a big bang with the first term you define. That is your first step into becoming a God-like figure.

Models for defining terms

My definition of _____ goes beyond the traditional assumption that _____.

However you fill in the blanks, you will be creating a unique cosmos. For instance, if you fill in the blanks with vocabulary from the last topic we discussed – dystopia – you will be creating just that – a unique take on dystopia.

My definition of dystopia goes beyond the traditional assumption that dystopias are bad, and utopias are good. An alternate definition of dystopia is a world that seems bad but in reality is the perfect place for the hero to enact her heroism. In other words, a dystopia is a utopia for one – in this case Katniss, and to a lesser degree Katniss' love interests and friends.

Sentences like these are cosmological in that they create new worlds for the reader. Before the reader encountered this sentence, dystopias were bad. But now they are good! His world has been rocked. This is heavy metal writing! We're not here to pump out five paragraph essays of mind-numbing milk toast and platitudes. We're here to rock the world. We're here to write like Gods.

What about the topic of nudity in public art?

My definition of art goes beyond the traditional image of the black cube in front of the corporate square. My definition of art is whatever provides us with a glimpse of transcendence, if only for a second. If for just a second we can be jolted out of our trance of quiet desperation and connected to the thread of consciousness that unites us all, then whatever it is, it's art. And if something with this power exists, the power to transport – then hell, yes, it should be put in public for all to share. If a glimpse of naked flesh is implied in the process, I think we can handle it. If art is just a window, anyhow, it can't be removed. You can cart away the object, but the epiphany has already been witnessed. It can never be unseen.

Another model for definition:

The essential element of _____ would seem to be _____, for example _____.

Another:

At its core, _____ from the basic need of humans to_____, and _____ can be seen a symptom of our fear that _____.

Look at the following for our topic of technology and communication:

The essential element of communication would seem to be the connection made between two or more beings. For example, a telephone ties you together by a string. The internet has allowed different iterations of this connection. But at its core, communication emerges from the basic need of humans to connect, and our worries about technology be a symptom of our own fear that the connection will be lost. We will be abandoned and alone on the steppe, on the plateau. The tribe will have moved on and we will be left alone. Never fear, Luddites, the tribe will not abandon you.

Another model, for our topic of neighborhoods shaping identity:

The struggle between _____ becomes crucial to understanding our terms.

The struggle between the stereotype and the authentic becomes crucial to understanding our terms. What is a neighborhood's identity? It might have an appearance to outsiders, as wealthy, poor, clean, ragged, but it also has an underlying authenticity, made up of the diversity within. No neighborhood can be pegged down or summed up in one phrase. Neighborhoods are too big. They defy generalization.

Whatever your topic, if you define the terms in this spirit of cosmology, creating a world from scratch, you will be taking a huge step to owning the prompt.

One more example:

Reparations: should descendants of African-American slaves be monetarily compensated for the crime of slavery that was inflicted upon their family?

My definition goes beyond the traditional assumption that it is all about money. At its core, the desire for compensation emerges from the basic need of humans to feel that their suffering has been acknowledged, that their pain has not been ignored. The call for reparations could be a symptom of how well or how poorly we're doing with race in this country. Either we've finally gotten to an okay-enough point where whites and blacks can sit down and openly discuss the matter. Or things have gotten so bad where we have tired of talking and have reached the point of "Just show me the money."

Now you try:

What about climate change? Is it real or is it a liberal SJW snowflake conspiracy to rob Americans of their industry and manufacturing jobs?

My definition of climate change goes beyond the basic assumption that _____.
At its core, the desire to confront climate change arises from the basic need of humans to _____ and _____ can be seen as a symptom of our fear that _____. The

struggle between _____ and _____ can be seen as crucial to understanding our terms.

BEYOND THE MODEL

Now you try, without any models. Write like a God. Create your own definition for the terms in the following prompt. Define your cosmos.

PROMPT:

Coates disputes the validity of the American Dream for people of color and/or minorities. Argue for or against the American Dream as you see it.

(Terms you might define: *what is the American Dream… what is American…. What is a Dream…. What are minorities?)*)

_____

_____
_____
_____
_____
_____
_____
_____
_____

Chapter Three

THE GOSH-DARNED THESIS

Now, you have done step one, by engaging at a deep level with the prompt. You have done step two, by defining the terms on your terms. Like a heavy metal rock star. Not like a hapless underling. You are ready for the third stage of this exciting journey: The Gosh-Darned Thesis. I call it that because this thing, the thesis, is undoubtedly something that you have been hearing about for years but never really found much use for, kind of like a guard dog that won't bark at intruders, or a water spigot that doesn't give you any water when you open it. That gosh-darned dog, water spigot. That gosh-darned thesis. Why have we had so much trouble with it?

One of the big problems with the way students are taught to formulate a thesis is that they are told to give away the farm – that is, to make their position perfectly clear. That seems to be a good idea, on first blush, but if we think of the world of our essay as a great Academy Award-winning film, for instance, we begin to see the problem with beginning the essay with a thesis that gives away the ending.

Spoilers ruin movies. Nobody wants to know the ending before they go to a film. So why do students give away the ending to their essays in the first paragraph? Why should anybody continue reading if we already know how the essay ends? We should think of the thesis as more like a movie trailer, which only advertises what is to come without giving away any spoilers.

It is true that students are not to blame for this amateurish mistake in writing. It is their high school teachers with their five-paragraph formula who mislead the students. Students have been taught to state their thesis in the first paragraph and then restate it in the last. No wonder student writing is almost impossible to read – there is nothing new under the sun in a high school essay.

Of course, even in college you might be penalized by some professors for not having a thesis statement in your intro. But even these conservatives will agree that the thesis should evolve throughout the essay. The only way for a thesis to evolve as you consider more evidence is for your thesis to be only partially formulated at the beginning.

Don't give away the farm. You have identified the main tension. You have defined your terms. Now you may state your inclination, or your best guess at how the essay might turn out. But don't overdetermine your results.

For example, in our essay about marijuana legalization, we have identified the tension of individual vs. group. We have defined perhaps marijuana as something you smoke, not eat like candy. So, it looks as though we are headed toward the conclusion that marijuana should be legalized but not in the form of edible candy, because that is dangerous to children. Thus, the thesis statement near the beginning of your article might read: if we are going to legalize marijuana we should be careful about how we do it.

A thesis is not a conclusion. Only after you have finished your essay, by bringing up various ways in which we need to be careful about legalization, do we state the results of our inquiry. "Thus, if we outlaw marijuana edible candy while coming up with some reliable method of preventing driving while under the influence of marijuana, legalization is a good thing."

This one simple distinction – that the thesis is different than the conclusion – seems lost on most incoming freshman writers. Even after learning the distinction, students tend to backslide and resort to this repetitive formula that they have learned – the five-paragraph essay where the conclusion repeats the thesis. It is comfortable. But it is not heavy metal writing. It is soft rock. What we used to call muzak. Elevator music. Heavy metal writers take their reader on a journey from thesis, through support, then through the gauntlet of opposing argument, accruing more glory along the way, until finally when they reach the conclusion there is a feeling of climax and closure. This cannot be done if you give away the farm in the first paragraph.

Show some restraint with your thesis. Think of it more as a statement of purpose than a statement of position. Your purpose is to stake out a position throughout the essay and finalize it in your conclusion.

For example, in the writing prompt about affirmative action in college admission, if you are going to argue in favor of affirmative action, fine. But don't give away your most compelling argument for affirmative action in your thesis statement.

Possible thesis statements in favor of affirmative action:

The affirmative action debate is not going to be resolved any time soon. However, there has been some movement recently in a particular direction. Notably, affirmative action has received support in some surprising quarters.

In the essay that follows this thesis statement you will reveal the surprising evidence that you have discovered.

In the paragraph below, you will notice the techniques of chapters one, two and three utilized effectively. First, the binary opposition (favoritism vs. inequality). Next, the definition of terms on my terms. (affirmative action can mean the same as legacy in white people). And finally, the statement of thesis that does not give away the farm (affirmative action is more complicated that it seems.) The thesis is written in bold below.

Affirmative action stirs up people's emotions on both sides of the debate. Some people think it brings equal opportunity to people, while others think it deprives people of that very thing – equal opportunity. There are other subtler objections, even among minorities. Some suggest that because of affirmative action, even after minorities succeed in getting into a good college, they must deal with the stigma that perhaps the only reason they made it in was favoritism to their race. Of course, the only reason a lot of white people made it in, too, might have something to do with favoritism. Perhaps they call it "legacy" – having a parent or grandparent who attended the school. **As we can see, affirmative action isn't as simple as it might appear.**

Yes, this is enough of a thesis. Now your essay can go either way, or right down the middle. Whatever side you land on, you are poised to take a mediative position that acknowledges both sides of the issue.

Now you try:

Choose one of the topics below and write a paragraph that uses the One Two Three method of beginning essays 1) dialectic 2) definitions 3) thesis that only partially answers the question of your argument. Then in space four, you will write the final destination of your conclusion, where your thesis is stated in full.

Topic: what is the most important thing to strive for in life? Some might say it is monetary gain, others might say it is career success. Perhaps it is making a difference in the world. Maybe it's just having fun. What is it that is really worth striving for, no matter how much effort it takes? Why?

Dialectic

_____

_____

_____

_____

Define terms: (hint: look at the term strive. Then look at the term important)

_____

_____

_____

_____

State partial thesis

_____

_____

_____

_____

Conclusion

_____

_____

_____

_____

Q. But aren't you supposed to take a side in your thesis statement.

A. You can take a side, or suggest a side, but you do not need to. It is sufficient that you frame the debate as establishment of your thesis. By the time your argument is finished, in the conclusion, your position will be made clear. It will be a position that evolves and does not merely restate and repeat itself. The more heavy-metal thesis statement is chock full of expectation, suspense and excitement. It does not answer all your reader's questions. Your reader will have to go on "the ride" to find out the answer.

Chapter Four

HOW TO DRAW A MAP

If you are to succeed in cosmological writing, you will create a world. Like any world, the way for people to know where they are going is – to use a map. Yes, even the creator of the world needs a map, or a design, to navigate his or her way around his own creation.

Now that you have your thesis defined in an adult, scholarly manner, with terms defined and dialectics identified, you are ready to take your reader on the journey to the conclusion. This journey is what scholars call your line of reasoning. A line of reasoning is made up of logical steps that follow one another in a particular order. These steps are premises or claims that must be proved, of course, by the supporting material you provide in each paragraph. The first thing you do is list all the claims or premises that you can think of for a particular thesis, and then arrange them on a map in the order that makes the most sense to you as an arguer. For example, for the thesis, legalization of marijuana will be good for our state, you might list the following reasons:

1. It will bring in tax money
2. It will free up the police and the courts
3. We won't have to put so many people in jail
4. It is helpful medically
5. Marijuana sales will provide jobs to people.
6. It is less addictive than alcohol or cigarettes
7. It is a free country and people should be allowed to do what they want if it doesn't hurt others.
8. The marijuana crop will help farmers make money.

After you write your list of reasons, claims and premises, you notice that some of the reasons go together in sets or groups. For example, reasons 1, 5, and 8 all have to do with economic prosperity. Reasons 2, 3 and 7 have to do with the justice system. Reason 4 and 6 have to do with medicine.

Thus, you can begin to map out a journey that takes you first through the economic reasons. At the end of the economic reasons, you would be able to transition to reasons that are more conceptual, while still having an economic component. For instance, freeing up the police has an economic element – policing becomes cheaper, but it also has a philosophical component, the idea that there are worse things than marijuana that police can concentrate on. This leads to the idea of number 7, that it's a free country. You have moved to a more philosophical, universal and deeper level. This is the direction that your train should head. From the specific, detailed, concrete, toward the universal basic principle. Finally, the medical reasons could be grouped together as a counter argument. If you anticipate the objection that people might have that marijuana is harmful, you can answer that with the counter that marijuana is less addictive (6) and that it actually is medically beneficial (4). Thus, you have arranged the train journey from thesis question (should we legalize?) to conclusion (yes, we should). To review, the categories move from:

I.   Material (economic advantage)

II.   Philosophical (freer society)

III. Countering objections (not harmful)

In chapter eight we go much further into part III, counter arguing. But already we have identified a three-step process for arranging our map of claims. Often a student will feel overwhelmed at the task of arranging a collection of supporting evidence. It seems he/she/they might start at any point on the list and proceed randomly. However, this is not the case. The human mind works this way analytically, from specific evidence to general principle. In terms of logic, this is called inductive. We arrive at our principles by examining the evidence, not vice versa. However, it is also deductive logic, in that we assume here that in our introduction the general principles and dialectics of the issue have been introduced. In other words, most essays are both inductive and deductive in their logic. The inductive/deductive question is an artificial distinction that writing manuals often make. An exclusively deductive or inductive argument is rather hard to find in the real world.

Now you try:

Here is a list of premises in favor of affirmative action in college admissions:

1. Affirmative action makes a more diverse population.
2. Minority individuals often do not have the same educational opportunity in elementary, middle and high school.
3. Minority individuals often do not have support at home for their educational ambitions.
4. Minorities are at a disadvantage in American society.
5. Affirmative action does not discriminate against whites because whites have more options and privileges
6. Affirmative action improves the education of whites because it allows them to be exposed to other viewpoints in the classroom
7. Affirmative action does not set up underqualified minority students for failure, despite what the opposition claims.
8. Affirmative action makes our society more just
9. Affirmative action will help rectify the inequality between the rich and poor

10. Affirmative action can be tweaked so that race and ethnicity are only one consideration among a holistic collection of credentials.

Please divide these claims into the following categories:

I. Claims that have to do with the disadvantages minority students face and the advantages that white students have.

II. Claims that have to do with making our society more just generally.

III. Claims that have to do with answering people's objections to affirmative action

Now that you have divided the claims into three categories, you can make a more specific map. Put the claims in order now, so that they form a logical line of reasoning, from your origin to your destination, from thesis question to conclusion.

1.

2.

3.

4.

5.

6.

7.

8.

9.

10.

Chapter Five

THE GOSH-DARNED SUMMARY

After you've established your dialectic, your definitions and your thesis, you are going to proceed to support this argument with examples, many of which will come from secondary texts that you have read on your own or in class. This supporting evidence, you can assume, has not been read by your audience, so to use it effectively you are going to have to briefly introduce and summarize the material.

In this chapter I am going to show you how to turn the most humdrum and unoriginal task of all – summarizing another text – into a creative event.

Students rarely spend enough time engaging with their own argument – so you can imagine they spend even less time engaging with the texts and arguments of others that they mention in their essays. Textual reference is often passing, minimal and ephemeral. But it doesn't have to be.

KEY ONE – BEGIN AT THE BEGINNING

I know it sounds obvious – it is. But when summarizing texts, and trying to give the sense of a piece of writing to an audience who hasn't had the privilege of reading it, it is absolutely essential to begin at the beginning, because where the author chooses to begin is that author's own cosmological moment – their "let there be light" statement. If you leave it out, you deprive the author of his or her own god-like power. For instance, in the following poem, the performance artist Kate Templeton, starts her poem off with a real bang:

Don't Freak Out
By Kate Templeton

Hey! Stop right there! Listen to me, you!
I been watching you and I see what's going on.
I know, I know. You're right in the throes
It's got ya. It's got ya by the short hairs
And there's nothing you can do.
Is there?
When all you can do is do what you can
Don't freak out, freak in.
When things go awry
Not according to plan
Don't freak out
Freak in
When nothing make sense any more
And everything spirals and spins
And you forget which way is up
Don't freak out
Freak in
Freak in until you find that spot
As warm and wet and dark and dank as the mud
And as cold and clean and cutting as the moon
Don't freak out freak in

And there inside your own game
You will grasp a loose string
And pull and pull with all your might
And bring the outside edifice down
Stand in your own space once and for all
Nobody can stop you
Don't freak out
Freak in
Time fell out of the back of the truck
And went cascading across the highway
Time came out of its Pandora's box
And there is no way you can put it back down now way
Don't freak out
Freak in
Freak in time
And out of time
Freak in the box
And on the highway
Smell the smell of the blacktop as it meets your mouth
They don't know who you are
They don't count
Only you count,
With your connecting eyes
Connect to me
And together we will fly
Across the freaky sky
Until this trip ends
Don't freak out
Freak in
With me.
Come on…

Perhaps we are using this text to answer the prompt: what is the best advice you can give to someone who is coping with difficult challenges in life?

Here are some ways to begin at the beginning.

1. In the opening lines of Templeton's poem "Don't Freak Out" she commands that we listen to her.
2. Stop right there, she says. Listen to me! As though she's accosting a stranger on the street. As though she's a lunatic.
3. Kate Templeton really wants us to listen to her. "Hey!" She says. That's a powerful hey.

Now you try:

Describe the cosmological moment, the beginning of Kate Templeton's poem:

_____

_____

_____

_____

_____

_____

KEY TWO: Proceed to the middle

After you have given the reader the cosmological moment, the inception of the text you are summarizing, your task is to remain cosmological in the second part of your summary. Remember, the second part of a text is birthed from the first, so just as much energy and forcefulness in writing is called for:

Now, to give the reader a sense of the next section of Templeton's poem, use the following models:

The idea of lack of certainty occurs for the first time in the next line where "everything spirals and spins."

Model: The idea of _____ occurs for the first time _____ when_____.

Next, Templeton proceeds to summon up human courage from the depth of the human soul, where you find solace in the spot as "warm and wet and dark and dank as the mud"

Next, _____ proceeds to _____.

Templeton soon sketches out an escape plan on back of the dirty napkin that is the middle of this poem: "Don't Freak out, Freak in."

(author's name)_____soon _____.

Now you try:

Describe Templeton's advice to sufferers in the middle of the poem. Hint, some words to use instead of writes: catalogue, enumerate, focus on, juxtapose____ with_____.

_____
_____
_____
_____
_____
_____

KEY THREE: This is the end!

It's important as you proceed toward the climax of the writing that you are summarizing to start bringing your own cosmological voice to the words of the author that you're quoting. That is, at this point emphasize how interesting your interpretation of the secondary text is. Remember, you are the rock star – they are just the supporting act. By the third part of your summary, there should be phrases like:

1. Templeton seems to be telling us to go within ourselves, but upon closer inspection connection with the other is clearly interwoven into the poem.
2. What these images have in common is pain in all its harshness. This does not necessarily imply masochism or reveling in the hardships of life. But it does imply accepting them. Again, it is the bravery that stands out in this connection. But Tempest also draws attention to the support of others, which is paramount in this struggle.
3. Essential to this portrayal is the notion of our helplessness in the face of time, which is stronger than any human. But we can stand our ground – together, by helping each other to not "Freak out."

To give the reader a full sense of the text you are using to prove your argument, giving the beginning, middle and the end is not a bad idea. Everything in the poem in fact can be fit into one of those categories.

Now you try:

Do a summary of an article of your choice, any piece of journalism, essay or non-fiction, where you use the models below to summarize the beginning, middle and end of the article. Hint: use some of the phrases from above, like: "essential to this portrayal," or "upon closer inspection." These are the scholarly grace notes that give your writing that superpower and super-strength. But vocabulary is only one aspect of this step. The more important task is being able to say in your own words what someone else is saying, without becoming passive and "studental". Remain egoistic and proud in your writing!

1. (Beginning)_____
   _____
   _____
   _____
   _____

2. (Middle)_____
   _____
   _____
   _____
   _____

3. (End)_____
   _____
   _____

_____

_____

_____

Sometimes you will be required to engage with a text in depth like we've been doing in this chapter. Of course, you have different length requirements and different expectations for your various writing assignments, and sometimes a more minimal system of quotation is more appropriate. But it is still possible to maintain a heavy metal level of engagement, even when quoting sparsely. That is what we will practice in the second part of this chapter.

CONNECT YOUR FIRST SUPPORTING EVIDENCE TO YOUR THESIS

The only reason to quote or summarize from a secondary text is to prove your thesis or support your argument. Sometimes students will do the hard work of quoting, paraphrasing and incorporating other texts into their argument, but then leave out the most important part – how that quote connects to your thesis.

For quoting, there is a three-step process that must be observed.

1. Introduce the quote and give the quote.
2. Say in your own words the meaning of the quote.
3. Connect it to your thesis.

As you can see, for one quote, that is quite a lot of material. You might be able to fill an entire paragraph, then, with just one quote.

For example, let's say our thesis is that courage is the most important quality to have in facing challenges of life.

If we want to use Templeton's poem to support this thesis, we must introduce Templeton, then give the quote, and follow up with the quote in our own words and how it supports our thesis.

1. (beginning) Templeton in "Freak In" provides ample evidence for the paramount importance of courage in facing challenges. "Stop right there," she says. "Listen to me!" As though she's accosting a stranger on the street. As though she's a lunatic. It takes courage to speak that forcefully. Perhaps she is giving the reader a little demonstration right off the bat about what it sounds like to live bravely.

2. (middle) The idea of lack of certainty occurs for the first time in the next line where "everything spirals and spins." Here she is saying that we can expect things to be challenging and confusing. This is exactly why we need to be valiant in our approach go meeting challenges.

3. (end) Templeton seems to be telling us to go within ourselves, but upon closer inspection connection with the other is clearly interwoven into the poem. "With your connecting eyes, connect to me, and together we will fly, across the freaky sky, until this trip ends." What does connection have to do with

courage? It is a risk, after all, to open yourself up to connection with another person. He/she/they might reject you. Here is where the bravery comes in.

Now you try:

Let's say that your thesis is that capitalism might have caused our climate change problem, but it might also be the thing that solves it.

1. (Beginning)_The author identifies burning of coal at the beginning of the industrial revolution as the first cause of rising CO_2 levels. However, he points out that some nations have already weaned themselves completely off coal. _____(Now connect that quote – how does that imply that capitalism is working to solve the problem?)

   _____

   _____

   _____

   _____

   _____

2. (Middle)_____The idea of capitalism reforming itself is presented with the example of the Exxon Mobil Corporation's green initiative. "The company, for instance, has pledged support for the Paris climate change accord." (Now connect that quote to the idea of capitalism working to solve the problem)

_____

_____

_____

_____

_____

_____

3. (End) What all these developments have in common is that they are inspired not by environmentalists but by American corporations. "Synthetic biology developed by such companies as Pioneer Corporation, Cobalt Technologies, Evolva SA, Gene Script Corporation, and **Exxon Mobil** also has a major contribution to make to green energy." (Now connect that quote to the idea of capitalism working to solve the problem).

_____

_____

_____

_____

_____

_____

Finding cosmological verbs.

In order to write with vigor, we must have vigorous verbs. Maybe as a student you have already been introduced by an English teacher along the way to a list of what are considered active, vigorous verbs. I have shown these lists to my students with limited success. Students get lost in a list of fifty verbs and it ends up not helping them.

It wasn't until I began to group effective verbs into separate categories, which I called fields, that I had any success in training students to write cosmologically. There are certain fields of human endeavor that lend themselves to this project of writing like a God. The visual arts, for instance, offer the writer a great method of conveying the mystical element of writing about ideas.

YOU'RE NOT JUST A WRITER – YOU'RE A PAINTER, A SCULPTURE, A MAD SCIENTIST, A SHAMAN, AN ALCHEMIST

The alchemist combines two elements in a magical formula to make gold. The way you prove things with your supporting evidence is by comparison, or combination of two alchemical elements in the process of forging an argument.

In writing books students are often introduced to the "compare and contrast" essay form, in which two things are examined closely for their similarity or difference. This form of essay is set as a specialized genre of essay as opposed to the several other ones that one finds in these texts: the definition essay, the cause and effect essay or the process essay. In reality, any essay in which a student tries to prove a thesis by bringing supporting textual evidence is in fact a compare and contrast essay, since the student will be comparing the textual evidence to their own thesis.

In other words, in our essay where we say affirmative action is a good thing because it makes our society fairer, we would look for evidence in texts which prove this claim. How do we know if a piece of evidence proves our claim? We compare it to the claim. Does the evidence compare favorably to our claim?

Here is a quote from a hypothetical text re affirmative action: "Minority students studied in inner cities are thirty four percent less likely to have only one parent in the home. With two parents in the house, obviously, there are double the resources to help students with homework and school responsibilities. By the time they get to college, it is no surprise that by conventional standards this student might seem less prepared or qualified."

Remember our first category of claim from the affirmative action map: claims that have to do with the disadvantages minority students face and the advantages that white students have.

Does it appear that our hypothetical text about the minority students having only one parent compares favorably with this category of claim? Of course. But more than that – the text provides a lens through which we can look out our claim and suddenly see the claim differently.

This quote suggests a different way of looking at affirmative action, not as an unjustified handout that is given to minorities, but as a profoundly compassionate gesture toward a disadvantaged child.

Here are some more ways of using the quote as a pair of heavy metal glasses to look at the thesis in new and exciting ways:

This suggests a way of reading affirmative action that questions our basic understanding of equal opportunity.

Looked at through the lens of a child's broken home, the heartlessness of the usual complaint against affirmative action becomes apparent.

The example of the single parent household sheds an instructive light on the heartbreaking lack of a level playing field among American homes that perhaps could be addressed by reasonable affirmative action policies.

The text offers an illuminating perspective on the human element of the affirmative action debate.

Pay close attention to these magical phrases: offers an illuminating perspective, sheds an instructive light. These scholarly phrases seem to bathe the argument in some kind of golden light. This is exactly what we mean by writing like a God. Notice that the imagery is borrowed from the painterly arts – shedding light. But we are not limited to painting. We can take a page from sculpture to make our essay artistic.

This quote refashions our view affirmative action, not as an unjustified handout that is given to minorities, but as a profoundly compassionate gesture toward a disadvantaged child.

This quote reworks our interpretation of affirmative action...

This quote reshapes our understanding of the basic circumstances of affirmative action...

Now, become a mad scientist in a secret laboratory with vials and beakers, a chemist mixing up an exotic comparison. Chemistry is a useful metaphor for the argument process. Just as scientists mix two chemicals to form a new compound in the lab, a rhetorician combines two ideas to form a third thing – a conclusion, a premise, or a claim.

This quote destabilizes our view of affirmative action as some kind of social justice warrior's handout to shiftless minorities. Suddenly we discover in the equation a living breathing human child.

The writer is a shaman standing between two worlds, the exotic world of ideas and the concrete world of things. Accordingly, the writer should use a vocabulary when making these exciting connections that underscores the mysticism of this gesture.

This quote extends our notion of what it means to be a human – suddenly affirmative action isn't about statistics, it's about a pulsating, terrifyingly poignant, human heart.

Imagine we wanted to connect the following quote to the thesis on affirmative action:

"The young Mexican-American student who arrived in this country at age 8, was stuck into a regular third grade classroom while not understanding the language. Did she receive "special treatment" at the expense of some white third grader? No. When she went home with her homework but neither parent was at home as they were both working two jobs to pay for their Los Angeles rent, did she receive special treatment then? When she was asked to work a part-time job after school and on weekends to help the family make ends meet, was she receiving special treatment then? In all three cases I think the answer is yes – she was receiving especially rough and unfair treatment. So suddenly at age 18 as she's somehow managing to fill out her college applications, despite all these odds that have been stacked against her all her life, suddenly now we are going to start scrutinizing her circumstances for some special advantage or treatment that she might receive at the hands of affirmative action? Shame on us."

I am going to give you now a chance to shine, to try your hand at painting, sculpture, mad science, and finally shamanism. Write like an artist, a rock star, a God.

1. Painting: use the verbs "sheds an instructive light," or "offers an illuminating perspective" on the issue of affirmative action, or "highlights" something about affirmative action, or "foregrounds" something that is not normally in the foreground of affirmative action. Then explain how it does that.

This quote_____.

_____

2. Sculpture: use the words reshapes, forges, recasts, refashions, reforms, or reworks the idea of affirmative action.

   This quote _____

_____

3. Mad scientist: use the verb destabilizes, reformulates, or crystalizes our understanding, reexamines, simplifies, etc.

   This quote_____

_____

4. Shamanism. Use shamanistic verbs like revolutionizes our understanding…. overturns conventional notions, opens our eyes to a new way of seeing something…

   This quote_____

_____

Here are some more interesting verbs for describing what a text says:

The example of the poor student **etch-a-sketches** an undeniable truth on the reader's mind – it's not a fair world out there.

The Mexican-American with no support at home **stars in an operetta with sad melodies** that cannot be denied by anti-affirmative action enthusiasts.

The author **tap-dances** around the issue of reverse discrimination by introducing us to a poor young student who has no support at home.

As you can see, these verbs all came from the performing arts. Now you try writing a sentence about this example of the immigrant student and affirmative action. For each of the categories below I will give you one sentence, and you create your own below.

Crafts

The following words are taken from lists of crafts and ornamental art. These words are useful because of the crafting with tools is a powerful metaphor for writing itself:

Crochet

Tattoo

Cross-stitch

Embroider

Etch

Spray Graffiti

Knitting

Weaving

Incise a hieroglyphic

For example, "The writer **cross-stitches** the idea of support from parents with the notion of support from government when it comes to education."

Now you try:

Use one of the craft words to make a connection between the specific example of the immigrant child and the general principle of affirmative action.

_____

_____

_____

Engineering

Engineering is another great metaphor for essay writing, whether it's civil engineering – building a bridge between two ideas – or something more exotic like electronic engineering – running one idea through a circuit of another idea and seeing what comes out, positive or negative. Here is a list of words culled from the technical language of engineering that might prove useful.

Analyze	Assemble	Build
Design	Examine	Identify
Interpret	Operate	Overhaul
Remodel	Repair	Research
Assemble	Assist	Design
Develop	Analyze	Apply
Direct	Establish	Modify
Initiate	Manufacture	Monitor
Inspect		

For example:

The author **examines** *the role of parental support in the equation of affirmative action.*

The author **assembles** *a case for helping poor immigrants based on the fact that they didn't have the same amount of help as youngsters that native Americans received.*

Now you try:

Use one of the engineering words to make a connection between the specific example of the immigrant child and the general principle of affirmative action.

_____

_____

_____

ACCOUNTING

Yes, even that driest of all fiends, number crunching, offers the artistic academic writer a unique system of metonymy with which to connect ideas together. What makes it exciting for the reader is to see the creative repurposing of these accounting tools to symbolize the process of calculation that goes into argument building.

The author **amortizes** over time the cost of helping an underprivileged immigrant become educated and **calculates** that it more than pays for itself when the cost is **reconciled** against future contributions the immigrant might make.

Now you try:

Use one of the following accounting verbs to connect the specific example to the general principal of affirmative action

Depreciates

Inventories

Investigates

Invoices

Adjusts

Allocates

Balances

Appraises

Administers

Audits

Indemnifies

Pays interest

_____

_____

_____

_____

_____

Another field that is considered dry and dull is that of the clerk, organizing files etc. This turns out to be perfect as a symbol for organizing thoughts. Look at the following list of terms from clerical work:

Clerical

Revised

Collected

Catalogued

Classified

Compiled Clarified

Indexed

Organized

Prepared

Processed

Simplified

Systemized

Here is an example of using a clerical term in the foregoing affirmative action context:

The author catalogues the various forms of underprivilege that are suffered in America – lack of education, lack of support at home, and lack of support when and if students do get to college.

Now you try:

Use a clerical term to perform the same rhetorical trick:

_____

_____

_____

Other fields in the arts and sciences might prove useful. In fact, look around yourself at your university. What specialized vocab can be repurposed in argument,

Botany

Fertilize – an argument or an idea can be fertilized, can't it?
Flower – an idea can flower into a bigger, more beautiful idea.
Germinate – An idea begins with a germination.

Now you try:

What word from botany can you find that might be useful in a metaphorical or figurative way? Can you make a verb from it? Try to use the verb in a sentence:

_____

_____

_____

_____

_____

Physics

Crystallize – to take a definitive form – i.e., an argument emerges in full form.

Accelerate – speed up, as in the example accelerates our understanding of the central principle.

Collide – Just as the planets collide, an idea collides with another, forming a reaction.

Now you try:

Collect some verbs from physics that might be useful in a metaphorical or figurative way? Can you make a verb from it? Try to use the verb in a sentence:

_____

_____

_____

_____

_____

Geometry

Invert – to turn upside down – i.e., an argument is overturned
Superpose – to place one thing on top of another.
Bisect – to split down the middle – a great verb for the mediative position in argument, i.e., finding the Golden Mean between two extremes

Now you try:

Collect some verbs from geometry that might be useful in a metaphorical or figurative way? Can you make a verb from it? Try to use the verb in a sentence:

Of course, there are many other fields in the arts and sciences from which you can draw inspiration as a writer – a truly creative writer, that is. Rather than hand them to you, I invite you to discover them for yourself by investigating the vocabulary of each of these other fields and coming up with words for each category that you think might be useful to you one day in constructing an argument.

The social sciences

Psychology, sociology, anthropology, history, geography, political science, linguistics, communication arts, philosophy, theology or religion., political science, economics, administration, entrepreneur, finance, etc.

The "hard" sciences

Thermodynamics, computer science, networking, automotive mechanics, aeronautics, medicine, zoology, astronomy, atmospheric science, oceanography, materials science, mathematics, microbiology, cell structure, etc.

Why do this?

What is the point of looking at all these diverse fields for inspiration in writing? The point is, it enriches the world, the cosmos, or your paper. For example, look at the following sentence, inspired by aerospace.

The author launches our understanding of Shakespeare into a whole new realm.

Suddenly, there is a rocket ship in your paper if you use the word "launch". This verb has invigorated quite skillfully the distinction we want to make about Shakespeare. We unconsciously get a little lift as we read this sentence, unaware that the lift is coming from this verb "launch", instead believing that the lift has come from the author's analysis.

Look at the following, inspired by the field of archeology.

We have unearthed various paradoxes at the heart of the pre-capital punishment position.

This verb "unearthed" makes the reader see for a moment the author in a *Raiders of the Lost Ark* hat, digging around a desert archeological site. The author has become an exciting character in this very interesting world – the essay!

Now you try:

The possibilities for enriching your textual world are really unlimited. Any field of endeavor, hobby, activity, or pursuit in the read world provides you with a resource – a cabinet full of specialized vocabulary that when applied to your text will transform it into something quite beautiful. So use your imagination and think of ten words from various fields of endeavor that have not been used in this chapter. List them here.

1.
2.
3.
4.
5.
6.
7.
8.
9.
10.

Now try to use these words in sentences that describe texts, ideas or distinctions in your essay: How you do this is up to you. You can write them directly into your essay. You can jot them down in the space below. It's a good idea to keep a notebook of verbs, which you use to collate exciting metaphors for scholarship as you go throughout your year. By the end of the year you should have hundreds that you can use to amaze and astound.

Chapter Six

THE SECRET TO ARGUMENT DEVELOPMENT

Your next task, after you have provided one supporting piece of evidence is to connect your next piece of evidence back to the thesis – and back to the previous evidence. Here the student is asked to develop an argument from his/her line of reasoning. And there is where the student usually stops because he or she has no idea what developing an argument really means.

When you bring up supporting premise number two from your road map, you will be doing more comparing. It will compare favorably to the idea of your premise. It will also compare favorably to the previous evidence, but it will not be the same as the previous evidence.

This is what is known as **development** of an essay.

Students are baffled to realize that this diffuse, amorphous and confusing technique – development of an argument – is little more than noting variation of evidence.

For example, regarding the thesis "Capital Punishment Should Be Abolished", we might have a roadmap that brings in these two premises as the supporting evidence:

1) Capital punishment does not deter crime
2) Sometimes innocent men and women are executed

These are two different "reasons" that both support the same cause. However, they are not identical. No two reasons are identical. That is why it is possible to develop an argument. If all arguments were identical, all essays would be effectively over after paragraph two. There would be nowhere for the argument to go. Noting the difference between reason number 1 and number 2 is an exciting part of the cosmological writing process because it is in these subtle differences between your supporting pieces of evidence that the subtle shading and forming of your piece of art will take place.

For instance, to support claim number 1 above, we bring in evidence from a study that shows crime is higher in a capital punishment state like Texas than it is in a state where capital punishment is banned, like New York. We have dutifully related that evidence back to our thesis, perhaps using some metonymy from the visual arts to jazz it up – "looked at through the lens of this statistic it becomes clear that execution is not working as a deterrent."

Now to transition to claim 2, we can rightly assume that simply providing support for claim 1 we have not already won the whole war.

ASSUME that your opposition is still fighting after supporting evidence number 1.

We must think, if it doesn't deter crime, what other reason might we have to keep capital punishment? One possible answer – retribution.

We have created the perfect opening for claim number two.

"So, what then is capital punishment working for? Perhaps it makes the family of victims feel better. Is this enough of a reason to keep it around?"

This feels like a transition that has been inserted between claim 1 and claim 2 that has led us to connect the two claims.

Weak transitions plague student writing. During our portfolio grading process that we do each year in the freshman comp writing program, one of the major points of distinction between a passing and a failing grade on our rubric is stated as "effective transitions between paragraphs."

To improve students' transitions, what do writing teachers do? They bring out another list, this time a list of effective transition words: furthermore, moreover, accordingly, etc.

Often students misuse these transition words. And oftentimes a little phrase like that is not sufficient to transition the thought – it merely transitions the syntax of the sentences.

Understanding the true nature of "transitions" helped me teach argument development and finally achieve an orderly line of reasoning in student argument with paragraphs that flow properly into one another. It is a huge revelation:

THERE IS NO SUCH THING AS A TRANSITION

As we can see from the above movement from supporting evidence number one to supporting evidence number two, the engine that drives the movement is not a transitional phrase. It is a much more powerful force than that. It is the engine of implied opposition. After every paragraph you should ask yourself, has the reader been convinced yet? And the answer should be no. We don't want the reader completely convinced until the end – why? Because we want the reader to keep reading.

In other words, all "transitions" are implied counterarguments.

Premise one – capital punishment is not a deterrent.

IMPLIED OPPOSING ARGUMENT – OK, it might not be a deterrent, but I still believe it's good.

IMPLIED SUPPORT FOR OPPOSING ARGUMENT – It might make families feel better.

COUNTER ARGUMENT – PREMISE TWO – Innocent people are sometimes executed. The risk of this injustice outweighs the potential benefit of feeling retribution.

Our final writing looks like this:

"Looked at through the lens of this statistic it becomes clear that execution is not working as a deterrent. So, what then is capital punishment working for? Perhaps it makes the family of victims feel better. Is this enough of a reason to keep it around? No, it is not, for one reason and one reason alone – sometimes innocent people are executed by our court system. For instance, DNA evidence has already cleared at least seventy people executed in the United States in the last twenty-five years. Capital punishment of an innocent person is a risk that outweighs the potential feeling of closure or healing the family of a crime victim might feel. Executing an innocent person, after all, would be compounding a tragedy with a travesty."

You have the following two premises for the thesis: women are still not treated equally or fairly in American society.

1. There are few women in boardrooms and high corporate offices.
2. Women are victims of sexual harassment in the workplace.

The two premises seem related – they are, after all, both dealing with the work environment. But your task is to find the implied counterargument after you have provided support for premise number one.

Imagine your reader saying, "I'm still not totally persuaded. I need more convincing." Write the transition to premise number two by answering this imagined objection.

But this discrimination is not limited to high corporate office. In everyday life in the workplace women are also discriminated against and harassed. In 2017 alone, there were over ten thousand cases of sexual harassment against women litigated in the United States.

(now connect back to your thesis)

Do men suffer the same degree of harassment and the degradation of a hostile work environment? No. Thus, we see that women are treated unfairly and inequitably in the workplace, from the bottom right the way to the top.

Now you try:

THESIS – The high percentage of African Americans in American prisons indicates a racist society.

Premise 1 – African Americans make up 54 percent of the prison population, but only 13 percent of the total population of Americans.

Premise 2 – Most African Americans are imprisoned for non-violent crimes.

Those are two interesting facts, but do they prove the thesis?

Development procedure:

1. Introduce the first premise.
2. Connect the first premise to the thesis.
3. Imagine an opposing view.
4. Answer the opposing view (counter)
5. Introduce the second premise.
6. Connect the second premise to the thesis

_____

_____

_____

_____

_____

_____

_____

_____

_____

_____

_____

_____

_____

_____

_____

_____

_____

_____

_____

_____

_____

_____

_____

_____

_____

_____

ADVANCED TECHNIQUES FOR THE SO-CALLED TRANSITION

While sometimes students incorrectly use "transitional phrases" in the topic sentences of their papers, another common error is transitioning from text to text. Often we will read a student paper that has the name of the next author and the next text in the first sentence of each paragraph. This is a red flag to professors. It shows that the student has not proceeded from idea to idea in a line of reasoning, but has rather proceeded from text to text, in what amounts to a survey of a group of texts. This is not an argument. It does not develop. It merely moves from text to text. Here is an example of what I call the "survey method of transitioning"

SURVEY METHOD
(or how not to do transitions)

In this paper, without reading the filler of each paragraph, you can see the student looks at bunch of well-known authors and analyzes how they look at the institution of marriage as compared to the poet Milton. The transitional phrases are in bold.

Marriage in Literature

Milton's piousness toward marriage is well-known, but it is not the only attitude toward British literature. An interesting contrast to Milton's piousness can be found in Plath's "The Bell Jar", which contemplates the meaninglessness of the institution of marriage. Lorem ipsum dolor sit amet, consetetur sadipscing elitr, sed diam nonumy eirmod tempor invidunt ut labore et dolore magna aliquyam erat, sed diam volup

Marital strife is a phenomenon **not only present** in Plath's "Bell Jar" but can be observed even more violently in her personal letters. Lorem ipsum dolor sit amet, consetetur sadipscing elitr, sed diam nonumy eirmod tempor invidunt ut labore et dolore magna aliquyam erat, sed diam voluptua. At vero eos et accusam

Where Shakespeare sees the hypocrisy of polite society as the cause of unhappiness, Milton turns to the weakness of the soul as the source of the problem. At vero eos et accusam et justo duo dolores et ea rebum. Stet clita kasd gubergren, no s

Other authors imagine a different approach. Blake presents in the narrative of "The Marriage of Heaven and Hell" an alternate way of viewing the mating ritual, not as a courtship between man and wife, but as a merging of various aspects of the individual soul. At vero eos et accusam et justo duo dolores et ea rebum. Stet clita kasd gubergren, no sea takimata sanctus est Lorem ipsum d

A similar theme emerges in Blake's paintings, which are equally personal and introspective. Consetetur sadipscing elitr, sed diam nonumy eirmod tempor invidunt ut labore et dolore magna aliquyam erat, sed diam voluptua. At vero eos et accusam et justo duo dolores et ea rebum. Stet clita kas

Elliot takes a similarly dim view of sexual relations. Consetetur sadipscing elitr, sed diam nonumy eirmod tempor invidunt ut labore et dolore magna aliquyam erat, sed diam voluptua. At vero eos et accusam et justo duo dolores et ea rebum. Stet clita kasd gubergren, no sea takimata

Quite a different picture of sisterhood emerges in Sappho. Nam liber tempor cum soluta nobis eleifend option congue nihil imperdiet doming id quod mazim placerat facer possim assum. Lorem ipsum dolor si

Other authors, most notably Shakespeare, imagine marriage in the Platonic sense of finding one's other half. Duis autem vel eum iriure dolor in hendrerit in vulputate velit esse molestie consequat, vel illum dolore eu feugiat nulla facilisis.

It is against this backdrop of war torn reformation England that we must place Shakespeare's poem about domestic squabbling and matrimonial "war." invidunt ut labore et dolore magna aliquyam erat, sed diam voluptua. At vero eos et accusam et justo duo dolores et ea rebum. Stet clita kasd gubergren, no sea t

We see similar dynamics in Sappho. invidunt ut labore et dolore magna aliquyam erat, sed diam voluptua. At vero eos et accusam et justo duo dolores et ea rebum. Stet clita kasd gubergren, no sea takimata sanctus est Lorem it amet.

We come to the heart of the problem with Elliot's "Wasteland." invidunt ut **labore** et dolore magna aliquyam erat, sed diam voluptua. At vero eos et accusam et justo duo dolores et ea rebum. Stet clita kasd gubergr.

IDEAS FIRST METHOD
(or how to do transitions)

In this paper, the student does not mention the next author until the second or third sentence of each paragraph. The new idea is what takes center stage at the beginning of each paragraph. This allows an argument to grow and develop from paragraph to paragraph.

Marriage in Literature

Milton's piousness toward marriage is well-known, but it is not the only attitude toward British literature. But this piousness of Milton's obviously is not so relevant to a modern skeptical age. The very idea of rigid moral standards strikes the contemporary poet as absurd and old fashioned. For instance, in Plath's "Bell Jar"….. Lorem ipsum dolor sit amet, consetetur sadipscing elitr, sed diam nonumy eirmod tempor invidunt ut labore et dolore magna aliquyam erat, sed diam voluptua. At vero eos et accu.

Marital strife is a very real phenomenon, not just a poetic conceit. We can observe from Plath's letters that… Lorem ipsum dolor sit amet, consetetur sadipscing elitr, sed diam nonumy eirmod tempor invidunt ut labore et dolore magna aliquyam erat, sed diam voluptua. At vero eos et accusam et justo duo dolo.

It may be the hypocrisy of polite society that is to blame for marital discord. However, the problem might be more internal than external. For example, Milton emphasizes the private human soul as the seat of tremendous battling between good and evil. Lorem ipsum dolor sit amet, consetetur sadipscing elitr, sed diam nonumy eirmod tempor invidunt ut labore et dolore magna aliquyam erat, sed diam voluptua. At vero eos et accusam et justo duo dolores.

Perhaps a different approach is called for. What if marriage is not a mating ritual at all, but rather, as Blake sees it, a merging of different aspects of the human soul? At vero eos et accusam et justo duo dolores et ea rebum. Stet clita kasd gubergren, no sea takimata sanctus est Lorem ipsum dolor sit amet. Lorem.

A similar theme might be visually represented as personal, introspective, quasi-expressionistic torment. Blake's paintings capture that very spirit. At vero eos et accusam et justo duo dolores et ea rebum. Stet clita kasd gubergren, no sea.

This dim view of marriage, it must be admitted, is fairly convincing. It is shared by Elliot, who…. Duis autem vel eum iriure dolor in hendrerit in vulputate velit esse molestie consequat, vel illum dolore eu feugiat nulla facilisis.

Quite a different picture of sisterhood emerges when we consider the possibility of erotic love in the same sex. While in the Elizabethan world, all the way up to the Victorian, the very idea was impossible, it wasn't always the case in the ancient world. Enter Sappho. Duis autem vel eum iriure dolor in hendrerit in vulputate velit esse molestie consequat, vel illum dolore eu feugiat nulla facilisis.

But perhaps marriage really is the miraculous discovery of one's other half. Shakespeare for one, believes it to be possible. Duis autem vel eum iriure dolor in hendrerit in vulputate velit esse molestie consequat, vel illum dolore eu feugiat nulla facilisis.

It is against this backdrop of confusion and mayhem in the bedroom that we must place any attempt to portray a marriage. Shakespeare had the added atmosphere of war-torn England to color his vision. Duis autem vel eum iriure dolor in hendrerit in vulputate velit esse molestie consequat, vel illum dolore eu feugiat nulla facilisis.

The dynamics of domesticity are consistent from age to age, and poet to poet. Duis autem vel eum iriure dolor in hendrerit in vulputate velit esse molestie consequat, vel illum dolore eu feugiat nulla facilisis.

The heart of the problem might be buried so deep in the human psyche that we will never perceive or communicate

it. Elliot made a valiant attempt. Duis autem vel eum iriure dolor in hendrerit in vulputate velit esse molestie consequat, vel illum dolore eu feugiat nulla facilisis.

Now you try:

Look at the way your line of reasoning in your premises is shaping up. Are you leading with the secondary texts and the other authors, or are you leading with your own ideas? Use the above example to model your own progression of idea as you move from paragraph to paragraph.

Chapter Seven

META DEVELOPMENT

By the time you get to the third supporting piece of evidence in your essay, your argument should be becoming at least a little bit self-conscious, or meta – writing about your own writing, commenting on your own commentary. Why is this a good thing? Because the more meta your writing becomes, the more apparent your personality as the God-like force behind the argument becomes. In other words, your writing becomes more cosmological. If there is an authorial presence, then the reader has more of a sense of a world with a Creator behind it.

Meta-writing introduces a new level of comparison. First, we learned to compare our first piece of evidence to the thesis. Then we learned to compare the second piece, and to note the differences between the second piece of evidence and the first. Now we are going to compare the third piece of evidence to the first two and to the thesis. But we are also going to compare what you are arguing at premise three to something else – to what you are not arguing.

Metacommentary clarifies what your point is by showing the reader what you are not saying. It situates your thought away from some more extreme possible interpretation.

For example, imagine for our third piece of evidence on capital punishment that we add the premise:

The methods of capital punishment are inhumane and cause prolonged suffering to the person being executed.

That's easy to connect to the main thesis. The constitution, after all, declares that cruel and unusual punishment is unlawful. If a prisoner writhes in agony for 22 minutes and smoke comes out of his ears as he is being executed, it's safe to say that we should outlaw capital punishment. However, there is a danger in this line of argument, for it implies that if we could find a human way of killing people that capital punishment would be acceptable. This is where we would insert our meta-clarification:

This is not to imply support for some other more humane method of execution.

Or...

I'm not saying that if we find a better more efficient chemical means of execution that I support capital punishment.

Notice that the first example of meta argument does not use the pronoun I. Some professors you will find prohibit reference to the first person in your essay. This rather old-fashioned regulation is going away in academia, but nevertheless the student should always ask a professor if he accepts use of the pronoun I or we. It is possible to be self-referential, as exhibited in A above, without using the personal pronoun. Both examples A and B move the argument in a self-referential way back to the thesis position, that all capital punishment should be outlawed.

Here is another example. In the argument on racism in America, imagine your third point is that while the prison population is predominantly African-American, the prison guard population is majority white.

This premise again supports the idea that the incarceration of African Americans is racist. However, it does present a danger: if we hire more African-American guards, would that make it ok that fifty percent of prisoners were African-American? Of course not.

A. This doesn't mean we should hire more African-American guards – that would do nothing to remedy the problem. The racial imbalance in the guard population does, however, highlight the racism in the system.

B. I'm not advocating hiring more black prison guards. What I am advocating is dismantling a racist prison system that is horrifyingly reminiscent of slavery in its racial dynamic.

Again, example A presents a meta-commentary, a clarification of what the argument is, without referring to the personal pronoun as in example B. Both are fine and accomplish basically the same thing – clarification and development of an idea, position or argument.

Now you try:

The thesis is legalizing marijuana. Our first two premises have given economic reasons. Our third premise gives a justice reason:

1. It will bring in tax money
2. It will provide jobs.
3. We won't have to put so many people in jail.

Write a meta-commentary about the state of your argument at premise number three. The goal of your meta-commentary is to swing your argument back from an extreme.

A.   Connect premise 3 to the thesis and/or the other premises.

_____

_____

_____

B. Write a meta-commentary that clarifies your views on premise 3.

_____

_____

_____

_____

Meta-comparison

As you arrive at your fourth piece of evidence you should be arriving at a central principle which informs all the pieces of evidence and proves your thesis.   This is an event that should not be taken lightly. What you have achieved is quite God-like. You have found a pattern that connects the four different, disparate things. You have sat like a sage on a mountain top and discerned the true nature of things. Thus, the way you express this central principle should revelatory -- cosmological.

Here are the cosmological steps one takes in arriving at the central principle.

1.   Find the astonishing parallel.

I would like to draw attention to the astonishing parallel between _____ and _____, in which both cases illustrate _____.

This is a meta-commentary that I call a "hidden pat on the back." After all, what is astonishing in this sentence? The parallel that you found. Therefore, who is astonishing? You are. Finally, the effect that this has on your text is guess what – astonishing! The reader who digests this meta-commentary begins to think of your own work as a bit out of the ordinary – astonishing in fact. In case you didn't know, professors give extra grades to astonishing papers.

Here are some more hidden pat-on-the-back models that you can use to find parallels that astonish:

Here we find a surprising analogy between _____ and _____.

Here the similarities between _____ and _____ are striking in that _____.

An interesting pattern can be discerned between _____ and _____, in which both cases illustrate _____.

A remarkable correspondence can be found between _____ and _____, since they both contain reference to_____.

Anyone who reads this paper will find it astonishing, surprising, striking, interesting, discerning and finally, remarkable. Each one of these adjectives, through the magic of meta-commentary, has named you, the author, as a mighty power, one to be reckoned with, admired, and greatly respected. The point of this ego, however, is not to build you up. It is to build up your world, the cosmology you created. You want your text shining and preening with this mystical light, because anything less is just boring, don't you agree?

2. Find some important difference between your pieces of supporting evidence. This will do two things – firstly, clarify the subtler parts of the argument and secondly, make you seem important!

This example may be seen as analogous to _____ but it is not identical to it. An important difference to remember is_____. Moreover, another distinction between the two is that _____.

Particularly significant is the fact that (in the first example) _____. In comparison, in the second text (some difference)_____.

Other than making your paper now "important" and "particularly significant", what has been added by pointing out some differences? Remember, these are the materials that you are working with as an artist – distinctions, subtle differences, correspondences and redefinition of things. These are the materials of your medium – essay writing. The way you organize and express them will always be unique to you. What I'm giving above are just models of the form you can use to create your own subtle, distinctive distinctions and correspondences as you develop your central principle.

STAND ON THE SHOULDERS OF GIANTS

Before announcing your grand central principle, it's important for you to pay homage to the great thinkers who have gone before you, but in this humble moment of acknowledgement, you will be sneaking in another cosmological distinction. You will show how your analysis goes further than the conventional understanding of things.

This notion both builds on and departs from the idea of _____.

What I am proposing is a more nuanced interpretation of _____.

A more sophisticated analysis of _____ will show that it is in fact_____.

But the more complex understanding of _____ is that _____.

Now your text, which was already astonishing, surprising, striking, interesting, discerning and finally, remarkable, particularly significant and important has become even more nuanced, sophisticated, and complex. We have arrived at the very epicenter of the heavy metal earthquake that is cosmological writing. Can you feel the earth shaking? I can. Here is the central principle.

After all this build up, it might seem like an anti-climax to arrive at a central principle that unites all your examples in support of your thesis. Don't worry, it won't be. When Beethoven finally resolves to the tonic after prancing from the dominant tone five times at the end of a movement in a symphony, we are finally brought home. Nobody is disappointed. The roller coaster ride is over for a moment – until the next movement begins. And never fear, our next movement *will* begin, as the opposing arguments come to challenge this, our sacred central principle. But for the moment we feel great satisfaction.

Ta da!

_____is the central principle that can be observed in all these examples.

The core idea at the center of this debate is _____.

The common feature of all these arguments is _____.

ADVANCED TECHNIQUES

In searching for the central principle, you have taken your readers on a voyage of ideas. Since you have identified a dialectic, two opposing forces, at the heart of your argument, it is likely that there is no simple solution to whatever problem you are exploring. This is why it is important not to eschew complexity. The following models allow you to search for your central principle in meta-commentary that embraces complexity and depth in unearthing an underlying truth.

1. Although it might seem that there is agreement about
   _____, it is clear form this broad range of stories about
   _____ that _____.

   Although it might seem that there is agreement about sexual relations, it is clear form this broad range of stories about men and women that there are two fundamentally different approaches. One….two…

2. It is not my purpose to come to any final conclusion, pronouncement, declaration, verdict on sexual assault gender relations men and women rape etc. But a common thread that weaves its way through all these narratives can be observed. The common thread is this: _____.

It is not my purpose to come to any final conclusion about the institution of marriage. But a common thread that weaves its way through all these narratives is the idea of trouble and strife overwhelming harmony and happy days.

Now you try:

Take one sentence from your draft and make it more complex by using one of the models above.

_____

_____

_____

_____

_____

Chapter Eight

ABC -- ALWAYS BE COUNTERARGUING

It is true that the ABC rule applies to the essay – she should Always Be Counterarguing, because it brings tension, conflict and interest to our argument. However, much of our counterargument should be implied, invisible, and structured into our transitions. It is not until we have arrived at a central principle that we should do a full on, explicit onslaught on our own argument.

There are four steps to the process of considering the opposing view:

Step One

Create a scenario in which the opposition is named, if only vaguely. The best antagonist in a Hollywood thriller might not even be seen until the end of the movie, but he is named -- I'm thinking of Kaiser Soize in *The Usual Suspects* or Bane in *Batman*. It's the same with opposing argument. Your opponent should have some sort of name. Even if it's just that – some:

Some might object that _____.

Conservatives will argue that _____.

Fans of classic rock might complain that _____.

Practice naming the accuser. Say you are arguing for, yes, legalization of marijuana. Your central principle that you finally arrive at is that it will make our society more open and less repressive. Who might object?

Religious groups might have the objection that marijuana will lead the population to the devil.

Mothers against drunk driving might complain that now there is going to be a menace on the highways that police cannot even identify with their breathalyzers.

Drug Abuse Treatment experts will tell you that more drugs are not what we need right now, as an opioid epidemic sweeps the nation.

Here is a vaguer, generalized, but still effective antagonist:

Some people might worry about the morality of bilking money out of the drug trade to fund our government.

Now you try:

Name some opponents to your central principle about affirmative action – that it makes our society fairer. Who might object to the idea of giving preferential treatment to minorities?

_____

_____

_____

_____

Step Two – Provide some support for the opponent's idea.

Really? Why would you want to help the other team? The answer is tension. The stronger your opponent is, the more tension your essay will have. The more tension your essay has, the more interesting it will be to the reader.

For instance, after stating above that "whites might object that it is reverse discrimination to allow less qualified students to take their places in American Universities," you might want to give an example of an aggrieved white student:

Gloria Gainesville was rejected from the University of Florida even though she had higher SAT scores than more than a hundred minority students who were admitted. She filed a law suit and won in Federal Court, who agreed that Ms. Gainesville was a victim of reverse discrimination.

Step Three – Make a concession.

If you concede some truth to the opponent's view, you are not losing the war. You are simply becoming more mediative, staking out a strong position between two extremes.

Indeed, it is true that some whites might be somewhat disadvantaged by the policy of affirmative action.

Notice that the language minimizes the damage done to whites ("somewhat disadvantaged'). Your concession can sneakily minimize or trivialize the opposition's concerns. That's a sneaky way of winning an argument.

Step Four – However.

Don't forget! No matter how much ground you concede to your opponent, you must follow the concession with the however clause that brings the argument back to your side. This is called the rebuttal.

However, the slight discrimination that whites might feel in college admission hardly impacts the overwhelming white privilege that exists in this nation. Calm down, white people. The ledger of advantage and disadvantage is still very much in your favor and probably will be for a long time to come.

Now you try:

Bring up an opposing argument that presents some challenge to the thesis of legalizing marijuana being a good thing. Follow the four-step process below.

STEP ONE – Name your opponents and state their objection:

_____might object that marijuana legalization will _____

_____

STEP TWO – Provide supporting evidence or reasoning for their opposing view.

After all, _____.

STEP THREE

Concede that there is some limited validity to the opponent's claim.

Indeed, it is true that _____.

STEP FOUR

Use the however to come back to your claim, while explaining why the opponent's somewhat valid claim doesn't take away from your main claim's validity.

However, _____

_____

As you can see, the four-step process can be boiled down to four introductory phrases 1) Some might 2) After all 3) Indeed 4) However.

Some might object _____ (insert the objection)

After all, _____ (insert the support for the objection)

Indeed, it is true that _____ (insert the concession to the objection

However, _____explain how your argument is nevertheless still valid.

Advanced Techniques:

There are certain scholarly phrases that clever arguers use to blisteringly dismiss their opponents. For instance, the phrase "withers under analysis" gives a great visual of the opponent's argument drying up and falling apart. Staying in the topic of marijuana legalization, imagine that the opponent has argued that marijuana smoking is as dangerous to the lungs as cigarette smoking.

However, these objections **wither under analysis**. *Principally, there is no conclusive study that links marijuana to lung cancer. Moreover, marijuana does not need to be smoked. It can be vaped, eaten or ingested in liquid form. So, while the health concerns might seem legitimate, they are not grounded in any empirical data.*

Try a few of these techniques to bring up and dismiss the objection to the thesis of climate change being caused by humans.

Climate change deniers might object that the temperature seems to be dropping, not falling, in many areas. After all, the temperature in our area last summer was colder than normal. Indeed, it is true that winters have been more severe as well. However, these objections wither under analysis. Principally, _____. Moreover, _____ (give two reasons to dismiss the objection)

Here are some super-scholarly sounding models that may inspire you for steps three and four. The following model concedes some validity but then quickly dismisses the objections.

His arguments notwithstanding, it is nevertheless true that

_____.

And yet upon further inspection, his argument falls short, since

_____.

These arguments do not withstand scrutiny, because

_____.

These local temperature changes **notwithstanding, it is nevertheless true** that globally temperatures have been rising.

And yet upon further inspection, the argument against climate change falls short, since a few minor micro temperature fluctuations do not change the macro evidence -- the world is warming up.

These arguments do not withstand scrutiny, because we can't judge the condition of the whole planet based on how it feels in our own backyard. That is what is known in philosophy as a hasty generalization.

Now you try:

Customize the models from the advanced techniques above to fit sept three and four of the argument against legalization of marijuana.

The argument may seem valid. There are several difficulties, however. Principally, _____. Moreover,

_____

His arguments notwithstanding, it is nevertheless true that

_____.

And yet upon further inspection, his argument falls short, since

_____

_____.

These arguments do not withstand scrutiny, because

_____

_____.

WHEN I SAY ALWAYS, I MEAN ALWAYS

Where should I put my opposing argument? Everywhere. Always be countering means you can counter after your first supporting evidence and you can keep right on countering. What every premise in your line of reasoning does, in fact, is question the warranting assumption of another premise – in an imagined opposition's line of reasoning. The easiest rule of thumb, of course, is to make your case as best as you can, then confront the opposition. But every point you make might be objected to.

Here is a way of countering objections by showing that the objection makes an incorrect warranting assumption. A warranting assumption is the basic truth that we must accept if we are to believe the premise is true. For instance, the warranting assumption of all people should have the right to vote is in our Constitution: all men are created equal. It is that principle that warrants the assumption that therefore all people should vote. Attacking your opponent's warranting assumption is like finding the chink in their armor and sticking your sword right in there.

QUESTIONING WARRANTING ASSUMPTION

CLAIM: Tattoos are symptoms decline of Christianity and return to paganism.

SUPPORT: Pagan societies had tattoos and piercings.

WARRANTING ASSUMPTION: Tattoos are pagan symbols.

ATTACK THE ASSUMPTION: This argument assumes that can only arise from pagan impulses. However, the attention on the paganism is misplaced because most people's choice of tattoo is based on highly personal, idiosyncratic reasons that have nothing to do with religion. In fact, often it's purely a fashion choice.

EXAMPLE: One question is: Can't we ween ourselves from dependence on oil and fossil fuels? Of course, to ask this question, the reader must accept fossil fuels are hurting the planet and that we need to switch from coal to solar. Lots of Americans don't accept that premise. Here's why they should:

MODEL: One question is _____? Of course, to pursue this question, the reader must accept the premise that _____ are _____. Some readers might not accept this premise. Here's why they should: _____

_____

_____.

Now you try:

Use the model above to question the warranting assumption of the following claim:

OPPOSING ARGUMENT: We can't force businesses to serve gay people because homosexuality might be against their religion. In America religious freedom must be respected.

Write a response to that argument that questions its warranting assumption:

_____

_____

_____

Chapter Nine

QUOTING COSMOLOGICALLY

Students often make punctuation or grammatical errors when it comes to quoting. Those are easy enough to fix. But the primary error students make when they bring in quotes is that they seem perfunctory when quoting – that is, it seems that they are happily filling three or four or even more lines of their paper with somebody else's writing, in order to not have to write the paper themselves.

QUOTES ARE NOT FILLER

The people you quote are the movie stars of your paper. What they say is their dialogue. You want their lines to be memorable, and let's face it, everything we say is not memorable. That's why, in order to write cosmologically, se have to be very selective with the lines we choose.

Only quote: 1) authorities and experts in their field, 2) extremely entertaining and original people, or 3) people who say it better than you can.

"But wait, my professor says I need at least five quotes in this assignment."

You can find five quotes, don't worry. But don't let the people you're quoting run your paper, even if they do satisfy one of the three requirements given above for quoting criteria. Even when quoting an expert, an entertaining person, or someone who says it better than you can, you must remain the God. How do you do that when quoting? You quote partially. I'm not talking about a block indented quote that takes up half the page. I'm talking about ending one of your own original sentences with someone else words that are in quotation marks. There is a huge difference between the two examples below.

A. The state of Colorado has received a great deal of revenue from marijuana. Paul Fellows of the Rand Institute writes, "Last year the State collected over $300,000,000 in marijuana related tax revenue. One quarter of that went to the cost of regulating and administering to the marijuana industry. A full three quarters went directly to the state budget. Some of the departments that benefitting were education, transportation, and health and welfare."

B. The state of Colorado has received a great deal of revenue from marijuana. Yes, some of the revenue goes to "the cost of regulating and administering to the marijuana industry," according to the Rand Institute. But over 2 million dollars has gone "directly to the state budget" to help fund social services and infrastructure needs.

Example B, as you can see, is a combination of direct quotation and paraphrase. Paul Fellows is not even mentioned by name in the second example. The author is the only name that matters!

QUOTING AND PARAPHRASING TECHNIQUES

As Schofield puts it in "Pro Hockey and the Problem of Facemasks, "_____".

According to Schofield in "Pro Hockey and the Problem of Facemasks," fans are not able to relate to hockey players as much as other pro athletes because of "recent imposition of facial protection systems."

As Strathern puts it, "being 'male' or 'female' is now a personal choice, not a life sentence." (14)

As _(author's name)_ contends (or claims, argues, avers),

"_____"

According to __(author's name)__ , "_____."

Now you try:

Imagine your thesis purpose is to question whether the political divisions are too strong in America and that we can no longer get along. Use the models to quote partially from the following paragraph:

"It is not easy to be a Democrat in a blue state, or a blue country for that matter. In my state there are some people who have told me it is their duty to God to save unborn children from abortion even if it means murdering doctors. Now, I am not an abortionist, but I am a physician. And a lifelong member of the Democratic Party. And a longtime supporter of woman's rights. Oh. I am also a man. Or am I? According to some of my conservative or evangelical or white nationalist or alt-right neighbors, I am a "libtard," a fool. It makes me want to move to California or New York. But Nebraska is my home. Why should the ignorance and hatred of other people uproot me and my family?" – Dr. Dan Stevens, MD.

According to <u>Dr. Dan Stevens of Nebraska</u>, "_____

_____"

(Now relate that quote to the thesis question of can we all get along?)

_____

_____

_____

_____

_____

ASIDES FOR PARAPHRASE

EXAMPLE: There was**, then,** a steadily increasing pressure on parents to get their children into pricey, prestigious pre-schools.

EXAMPLE: Such web sites and apps**, this logic goes,** have more to offer the ordinary user than the free offerings one finds on the cable channel or the Windows home screen.

EXAMPLE: Some people might claim TV is just for entertainment. These kinds of clownish portrayals**, this logic goes,** shouldn't offend us, they should make us laugh.

Now you try:

Put the following quotation into the paraphrase model where you explain the logic of the quoted claim.

John Andrews, from the Space Administration, says, "I'm not sure we should be sending signals into outer space. After all, how can we be sure that they won't be heard by predatory species who will come to earth and harm us. Or worse, eat us."

John Andrews, from the Space Administration, questions whether we should be sending signals into space, because the universe might not be such a friendly place. _____, this logic goes, _____.

Chapter Ten

YOUR CONCLUSION IS THE REAL QUESTION

By the time you have gotten to your central principle and applied an opposing argument to test the mettle of your central principle, you have come a long way on your journey toward your conclusion. In fact, you are almost there. Your thesis has evolved from its humble beginning as a dialectical question with terms defined by you. It has met along its way the first piece of supporting evidence, then the second and the third piece. All of these pieces of evidence have been placed in relation to one another in your work of art, the multi-dimensional moving sculpture that is your paper. The central principle emerged like a newborn infant from these birth pangs, and immediately encountered the resistance of the opposing view. It emerged stronger, baptized by your thought, arising toward the last section of your essay.

During the denouement of your conclusion, the battle is over. You are not going to fight or compare or contrast or make any more arguments. But you are going to take us even deeper. Here is a model:

There really is not much more to debate about the issue of
_____. The real question is_____
Will_____? To answer this question, _____.

Imagine that you have convinced the audience of the wisdom of legalizing marijuana. You have gotten to your conclusion by battling the opposing argument that marijuana is going to somehow threaten our public or private safety. But you've proved that those are unnecessary worries. The central principle that emerged from all of your examples was that we can transform a problem – drug enforcement – into an opportunity – raising money through taxes on sales of marijuana. Now you want to leave this war behind. It was exhausting, after all. That is where the real question comes in.

There really is not much more to debate about the issue of marijuana legalization. The real question is being we willing to take the gamble? There is no guaranty that the legalization of marijuana will be without hiccups. In fact, there are guaranteed to be problems implementing a change as massive as this one. The real question is, is it worth the risk? To answer this question, we should look perhaps at the worst-case scenario. What if more legal drug use in our society leads us down a path of unproductive and pleasure-seeking delirium? What if our state becomes chaotic and crazy and dangerous? What if stoned drivers lead to traffic fatalities throughout the state, and young children are poisoned accidentally by attractive looking edibles that they mistook for candy? It sounds terrible, it must be admitted. But if that worst-case scenario takes place, we as a state could easily vote to make marijuana illegal again. And the worst-case scenario could be bettered. However, think of the best-case scenario. What if because of legalization young people's lives are tainted forever by the scar of a conviction for a drug offense? What if they are able to go on to become successful professionals, join law enforcement agencies, sign up for the armed services, and generally contribute to our society. Think how many families have been ruined by the intervention of the law enforcement system due to the possession or sale of weed. Think how many families would be saved from potential disaster by legalization. Can we afford not to take that risk?

This essay has ended very differently than it began. In the beginning it was just a question, should we legalize the drug. Then it became a dialectic – government control vs. individual freedom. Through the examples of economic advantage and more fair treatment of citizens, an argument formed that supported the idea of legalization. At last a pattern was discerned in all these examples which lead to the formation of a central principle – the pursuit of happiness. All of the supporting examples from our map shared this characteristic, that marijuana legalization in many ways will lead to more happiness for people. An opposing view was presented, that it was unsafe to legalize dope. However, these doubts were answered with other supporting evidence. Finally, we are ready for the real issue. The question under the question of marijuana legislation – is it worth the risk? The cost/benefit equation is the real question. It's the practical concern. It is what we must ultimately face if we make the decision to legalize marijuana. And its answer is uncertain.

Your conclusion should not give the final answer on things, but it should point in the direction you think things are most likely to go.

Now you try:

You have followed through this book the various stages of developing an argument in favor of affirmative action. The map looked something like this:

1. Dialectic – favoritism for minorities over privilege of whites
2. Thesis – affirmative action seems to make society more equal.
3. First support – smaller percentage of minorities are able to gain admittance to, pay for, and graduate from college.
4. Second support – public schools for minorities do not do as good a job preparing them for college as public schools for whites.
5. Third support – in the home, minorities do not find the same level of support from parents and other relatives for their education.
6. Opposing view – but it's unfair to a white student who is more qualified.
7. Answer to opposing view – whites still have plenty of privilege

8. Central principles – equality of opportunity – the level playing field. The American Dream.

Now it is up to you to arrive at the real question regarding affirmative action, the question that goes even further than the parameters of this rather small question – should race be considered in college applications – to something much bigger and more universal and more compelling.

What is that question?

_____
_____
_____

Try to answer that question.

_____
_____
_____

Chapter Eleven

REWRITING

The Cosmological Peer Review or Self Review Sheet

After your first draft is completed, often in academic writing classes you submit it to your peers for review. Professors like this because it is literally a day off for them – they don't have to teach on peer review day. They just sit back as the "guide on the side", no longer the "sage on the stage," as the students tear each other to pieces.

No.

That is not useful. What we've created in our first draft is a world, remember. It's a living, breathing entity. We don't want to sit in judgement of that world. We want to enter it.

The first step in the Cosmological Review, whether you are reviewing someone else's draft or your own, is to enter the world.

How do I enter the world as a reader?

Look Around

What is the first thing you do when you enter a world – say Disneyland, or Six Flags? As soon as you walk through the gate you begin looking around expectantly at the attractions, trying to decide which one to approach first. You might take the whole scene in, amazed at what a wonderworld you've entered.

That is the attitude you should have when reviewing a draft, whether it's your own or someone else's writing. Don't begin reading the paper looking for mistakes. We don't go into Disneyland checking for typos in the signage, do we? No, we have better things to do with our attention.

Remember, the "attractions" in the world of the essay are the distinctions. That is the technological marvel. That is the purpose – to provide beautiful distinctions of argument.   So, look around and begin spotting those. The first thing you might see as you go through the gates is the attention grab. Did that grab your attention in an effective way? Yes or No. What about the dialectic? Remember, from Chapter one? Did the writer identify the opposition of forces in tension with one another that lies at the heart of the writing prompt?

Simply answer these peer review questions with the yes or no and explain your answer in the blank provided.

Did the attention grab succeed in grabbing your attention? Yes or No?

_____

_____

_____

Was the dialectic at the heart of the prompt revealed successfully? Yes or No?

_____

_____

_____

Did the author define his/her/their terms in an effective and original way? Yes or No?

_____

_____

_____

Was the gosh-darned thesis presented in a way that did not give away the farm, yet presented the purpose of the essay? Yes or No?

_____

_____

_____

Was the map correctly drawn or did you get lost in this amusement park as you attempted to follow the line of reasoning? Yes or No?

_____

_____

_____

Support – was the supporting evidence related back to the thesis? Yes or No?

_____

_____

_____

Was the supporting evidence related to the other pieces of supporting evidence so that a pattern begins to emerge? Yes or No?

_____

_____

_____

Did that pattern lead to a central principle? Yes or No?

_____

_____

_____

Were the quotes and paraphrases done cosmologically and correctly? Yes or No?

_____

_____

_____

Was there sufficient counter argument, concession and rebuttal? Yes or No?

_____

_____

_____

The deeper issue – was it established in the conclusion? Yes or No?

_____

_____

_____

HOW DO IMPROVE MY PAPER?

Your first draft has created a world. This world, this cosmos, is centered around a dialectical struggle between two forces. In this world there are many beautiful things to see. These beautiful things are the distinctions that you were able to make, eloquently, provocatively, between the various elements that supported and attacked your argument.

The second draft is another cosmos, a place where a great meeting will take place, between the reader and the author. Only this time it's even better. There are two levels of improvement that take place in the second draft:

A) Argumentative improvement
B) Cosmetic improvement

The argumentative improvement takes place on the level of the line of reasoning. In the second draft you examine where the argument is weakest, and you strengthen it. We will work on that in a minute.

The cosmetic improvement might not change the basic argument all that much, but it makes it much more polished and finished. You have already built the house. But now you paint the walls and tile the floors. Only then will you invite the public in to inspect your edifice. The techniques of cosmetic improvement will be explored in the next chapters. These techniques can of course be used while writing your first draft as well, but they are especially useful in the finish carpentry session that takes place in the second draft.

Identifying the weak spot.

After seventeen years of looking at weak first drafts, I found that all the argumentative weakness boils down to one of two categories. Either I) there is not enough specific evidence or II) the specific evidence is not related back explicitly to the thesis -- in other words, it proves nothing.

Category I – not enough specific evidence.

If your paragraph is too general, you have spent a whole paragraph talking about principles or ideas without one specific example to let the reader know what you're talking about exactly. To remedy this, after you have found an example that applies, use the following sentence structure:

A great example of this _____ is found in

_____

_____

_____

A specific instance that proves this_____ is when

_____

_____

_____

There is much evidence of this _____ in the world.
Perhaps the most compelling is _____

_____

_____

_____

Here is a too-general paragraph about the ideas of equality as they
relate to racism in America. Use one of the above models to provide a
specific example.

      American society is homophobic. People don't want to
accept gay people as the same as them. People are afraid of gay
people or they hate them. It is because gay people are different
from them. They only see marriage as between a man and a
woman. Some people say it is the Bible. Some people say that
gay people are unnatural. None of these explanations are real.
They are just bigotry.

_____

_____

_____

_____

_____

_____

_____

_____

FIND MORE CONTRASTING EVIDENCE

Perhaps the weakness of your essay is that it does not quite succeed in convincing the audience of your main point. Never fear. There is an infinite amount of evidence in the universe, according to the latest theories of physics. The evidence you need might not be in your paper yet. But you can easily move it there.

I think it's always a good idea to add a new source or a new textual quote to a second draft, because it adds to your engagement with the process. Do you remember the first chapter on engagement? Rewriting is not, after all, just tinkering with a comma here and there. It should be approached as an equally important step in the process as drafting your essay. You want to engage fully in this stage of writing, too, and forcing yourself to add more text is a great way to do just that. Perhaps you have page limits and will have to subtract text in order to find room for the new items. That's a good thing. Even if it means killing some of your darlings (some sentences or paragraphs you loved from the first draft) we are ruthless in our engagement. My favorite type of evidence in the second draft to add is evidence that contrasts somehow with your previous evidence yet proves the same point or central principle. This is more interesting to the reader than yet another piece of evidence that chimes perfectly with all the other evidence. The oddballs are always the most interesting characters in fiction, aren't they? Create a little oddball piece of evidence for your second draft, in order to improve the flavor of your argument.

Here is a list of sentences used for contrast and difference.

DIFFERENCE

1. (Something in the first text) undermines (an idea presented in the second text) by emphasizing _____.

2. The (newer text) refuses to, fails to, denies, resists, does not perform _____ which its antecedent, (the first text) demands, celebrates, claims, posits etc.

3. What becomes clear from close-reading of both texts is how (one text is more complex, more interesting, more nuanced, more sophisticated, more intelligent, more modern, more engaging, more accurate than the other text). The _____ in (the first text) is striking, (clear, undeniable, ever-present, highlighted) whereas in the (second text) _____ (some difference)

4. Particularly significant is the fact that (in the first text) _____. In comparison, in the second text (some difference) _____.

5. In effect, the second text provides more, greater, stronger, richer_____.

6. The _____that is granted in the first text is withheld in the second.

7. ...gives a different perspective on....

DEVELOPMENT

As your analysis moves along, each new element both builds on and departs from the previous ones.

1. This text both builds on and departs from the idea of ____.
2. The second text extends the notion of _____ to_____
3. …. reiterates this notion of _____ in the story of

    _____.

4. …. develops, rewrites, reinvests, reworks, reconsiders,
5. What is important to remember, however, is that in the second

    text _____ whereas in the first text

    _____. Both authors had distinct

    _____and were influenced by distinct

    _____.

6. This text puts a different gloss on that text which emphasizes

    _____ rather than _____.

7. *Example:* Adele de Senone is an interesting variation on the theme: the sweetness of the couple and of the young man who loves …

    _____ can be read as an interesting variation on the

theme of _____.

Let's say you already have an essay with four premises proving capital punishment is wrong:

1) It doesn't deter

2) It sometimes kills innocent men/women
3) It is racially biased
4) It is cruel and painful

Now you have an interesting piece of evidence you'd like to include in your second draft. It's different than all the other pieces of evidence. It supports an added premise – that despite what we've heard, executing the killer does not make the victim's family feel better. This evidence is an article with interviews of several family members who felt that the capital punishment did them no good. If anything, it made them feel worse. This is a very different piece of evidence, because it deals with a specific murder and a specific murder victim's family, and their feelings. It does not talk about the justice for the victim.

Here we use sentence number 5 from the Difference list above:

In effect, this text provides even stronger evidence against capital punishment. It's not making anybody feel better, so why don't we just quit it?

Or use sentence number 6 from the Development list above:

This text puts a different gloss on the whole question of state killing of convicts, undermining one of the main purported benefits of state murder – that it makes the families of the victim feel better.

Now you try:

Use another sentence from the lists above to connect the evidence of families not being made to feel better by capital punishment to the other arguments against it.

CATEGORY II – evidence not related back to thesis, therefore proves nothing

I remember at one of our portfolio grading sessions I was sitting there reading a paper written by a student of one of my colleagues. Looking back at the early drafts of the paper I kept seeing in handwritten red pen, "Proving?" Whenever a piece of evidence was presented, but not related back to the thesis, the professor would write "Proving?" I looked at the next draft. Wherever he had written "proving?" earlier, the student now had successfully stated what exactly it was that the evidence was proving.

I began adopting that same simple comment – proving? – in my own teaching. It is very clear, and the students respond well to it. If the evidence proves nothing, it doesn't belong in the paper. It serves no function.

For instance, let's look at this paragraph about suicide prevention that brings up the example of Hamlet.

Suicide prevention is not easy. "To be or not to be," said Hamlet. "That is the question, whether it is nobler in the mind to suffer the slings and arrows of outrageous fortune…" Hamlet struggled with the idea of suicide. He wasn't sure if he should fight or if he should give up. Ultimately, Hamlet did not commit suicide. He was killed by Laertes.

I might write "Proving?" on this paragraph in the margin. It is interesting that the student brought up Hamlet as an example. However, it has proved nothing. In fact, Hamlet is not even talking about suicide. The speech is about his indecision and inability to act in taking revenge on his uncle. But never mind. It can still prove something.

We are not a court of law, after all. There is no parliamentary procedure or legalistic rules that we must abide by in rhetoric. In rhetoric, anything can be used to prove almost anything else. Why? Because rhetoric uses one piece of evidence or text as a lens to look at a question, not as a judicial end in itself, but as a tool for seeing.

Nobody can be convicted and imprisoned by an essay. But something can be seen.

One of the best ways to make a piece of textual evidence prove something is to use it as a lens, a telescope, a pair of binoculars, a mirror, a way of looking at something else. This is the phenomenological use of texts as lenses to look at another thing. For instance,

Hamlet with his "To be or not to be" soliloquy suggests a way of thinking about suicide that interrogates the very nature of death itself.

Shakespeare with the character of Hamlet gives us a way of reading the contemplation of suicide not as a plea for help but as a serious philosophical inquiry.

Looked at through the lens of Hamlet, written five hundred years ago, the question of suicide prevention becomes at once more daunting – it's been around for millennia as an issue, so it's probably not going to go away just now – and more hopeful – after all, Hamlet decided it was not a good idea to kill himself. He worked it out.

Now you try:

Take this paragraph where the evidence is not tied to the central thesis and use one of the model sentences above to let it illuminate your thesis in some way.

There were lots of cases last year where people's religious beliefs clashed with LGBT rights. In Oklahoma, a plumber left a house when he discovered the owners were gay. He left the leaking pipes that he had been contracted to fix. By the time the owners got home the house had been flooded. They filed a lawsuit and won based on the equal protection clause of the Constitution. When they came home they expected their pipes to be fixed – not their home flooded. The Court did not believe that it was responsible for the plumber to behave that way.

Rewrite the paragraph but tie the example back to the thesis/dialectic of religious beliefs conflicting with LGBT rights.

_____

_____

_____

_____

_____

_____

_____

_____

_____

CLARIFY WHAT YOU MEAN
Enumerated and Non-Enumerated Lists

In the second draft, you might have loosely tied your evidence to the thesis. But now is the time to fill in the gaps and the details and clarify exactly what you mean with your argument. For instance, in the examples above I touched on how Hamlet is tied to the theme of suicide prevention. However, it's only a loose connection. Using meta-commentary and the technique of listing, I below clarify what I mean with this connection:

"There are two aspects of the soliloquy that I would like to examine in order to clarify what I mean by this way of reading Hamlet. First, the use of the infinitive, to be, rather that I am indicates a universal questioning of the kind that philosophy makes, not a personal cry for help. Second, the use of article the with the noun question. The question. Hamlet doesn't say, 'That is a question that has been bothering me.' He says it's *the* question, implying the only question, and then he stops, indicating that it is not just the question for himself, but for all mankind. What does this prove about suicide hotlines? They are not just for crazy, disturbed people. Suicide is a possibility, an option, a question, for all mankind."

Listing is often found in academic writing and in speechifying. It makes the speaker or the author seem very in control of his or her material. It proves, for example, that he's not making it up as he goes along. He's done his homework. He knows, for instance, that there are three ways that the point he's making relates to the other point he's making. 1. Bla bla bla. 2. Blab la bla. (Now build to a climax). And perhaps most importantly, 3. Bla bla bla bla.

This is second draft material, why? Because in the first draft you *were* making it up as you went along. Yes, you had a map, but now you can see everything more clearly. You are capable of not just tying the evidence of the thesis in one way, but in myriad ways. And these ways you will list, in a scholarly fashion.

We have already been introduced to this list in the opposing argument section:

Principally, this bla bla bla. (Give the most important point about the evidence). Secondly, (bla). And finally, (give your last point.)

I find "principally" to be more effective than "first", because it just sounds more scholarly.

Another version of this is "primarily".

Primarily, this evidence bla bla (give the primary point.) But, additionally, (give the ancillary point).

Now you try:

Take this evidence which in the first draft is connected back to the thesis, but only weakly. Now, in the second draft, connect it back to the thesis three ways, in a list with the most important way beginning or ending the list.

Enumerated list:

There are several ways (in which the evidence relates to the thesis). One, _____. Two, _____. But perhaps the most (fascinating, important, interesting, remarkable, significant) connection is_____.

Non-enumerated

There are a few important ways that this evidence resonates. Primarily, _____. Moreover, _____. Furthermore, _____.

Chapter Twelve

COSMETIC SURGERY

In order to create a great scholarly work of art, you must take advantage of certain scholarly conventions that are used by the masters. This is done in any art form – Da Vinci used conventions that had been established in the Baroque age by painters like Giotto. Picasso used conventions in the 20th century that had been established by El Greco in the 16th century. These scholarly conventions are tried and true techniques that will make your cosmos seem just that much more scholarly and wise and delightful in style.

You wouldn't want to use these techniques consciously during your first draft, because that is the venue for wrestling with ideas, not style. However, the more you study and practice the following cosmetic scholarly techniques, the more they will become internalized and you will use them unconsciously at all stages of the writing process, not just re-writing.

Put in Four Magic Words

We've already been introduced to the mystical power of certain words to subconsciously elevate your tone. Scholars do this more and more as they gain confidence in their own scholarly abilities. They have begun to find the whole process of research and writing as such an amazing activity that it begins to exude out of them as they write.

Here are four sentences for four of the most magic words – extraordinary, astounding, significant and shocking.

YOU ARE AN AMAZING, UNIQUE AND BRILLIANT THINKER

EXAMPLE SENTENCE: So there is an **extraordinary** convergence here between Stirner and Lacan.

Let us analyze what is really happening here. By using these structures and these adjectives, you have presented your ideas as cutting-edge, new and exciting. This novelty is what professors want. They don't want stale bread. They want fresh-baked, original thinking.

YOUR FINDINGS ARE ASTOUNDING!

This notion of _____is **astoundingly** _____ (adjective)_____, in that _____ (explain why it is that adjective).

YOU ARE SO SIGNIFICANT!

This is why _____ is **significant** for our analysis:

_____

YOU ARE A SCIENTIST WHO HAS DISCOVERED A SHOCKING RESULT!

So there is **a shocking** _____(either compare two things or point something novel out about your subject).

Now the trick, of course, is that the "content" of your analysis needs to live up to this "form" of scholarly exuberance. This exercise is only a beginning – it invites you to think that it is actually possible for your writing to rise to that level.

After you have done the hard work of a first draft, it is quite likely that some of the distinctions you have identified in your argument are quite extraordinary. Find four places in your first draft to use these terms.

INTRODUCTORY PHRASES
Make A Super Scholarly First Impression.

Paradoxically; To be sure; More fundamentally; Alas; To be clear; etc. With these sophisticated calling cards, you and your sentences will be invited into the most exclusive salons and private scholarly clubs in town. Just kidding. But, truthfully, these scholarly sounding introductions are one of the techniques scholars use to let their audience know that they are just that – scholars! It is a little bit like a secret hand-shake in the scholars' club. It lets your audience know that you are playing this game at a certain level of sophistication, and that they can expect an intellectual ride as they read this paper.

Here is a list of introductory phrases.

INTRO PHRASES

To be clear, these aesthetic qualities of surprise are not found in every TV show, just the best ones.

More specifically, various anti-depressants are purported to alleviate depression and anxiety, although there is scant evidence that they can treat OCD successfully.

On the contrary, these products contain more petroleum than gasoline itself.

Furthermore, there are many reasons to disqualify a juror other than political affiliation.

In short, Americans don't trust the media as much as the media thinks they do.

Of course, there are lots of reasons to doubt politicians.

Thus, the attitude of police toward minorities has not changed.

Moreover, the study of endangered mammals gives us plenty of reasons to worry.

Again, the climate is becoming more extreme in Halifax.

It follows that secretaries should not sit at their desks all day because sitting is the new smoking.

In straightforward terms, true-crime novels are murder porn.

In particular, after the age of seventy people lose the ability to learn a new language to fluency

Indeed, everything points to the opposite conclusion.

Likewise, it must therefore be true that lifestyles have changed in the past twenty years.

Nonetheless, life does get better for the diabetes patient.

Still, not everybody makes dining out into a way of life.

To be sure, much of what we know about this Sumerian New Year festival comes from the following account of the rites.

In sum, the Italians were not lagging in military equipment.

Besides, Chamberlain didn't believe Hitler would invade Czechoslovakia.

Not surprisingly, he did.

In other words, Chamberlain was a fool.

Consequently, my Grandfather enlisted and was killed on the beaches of Normandy.

Paradoxically, I am named Norman.

Hence, I blame appeasement.

At the same time, we must not forget that hindsight is 20-20.

More fundamentally, the activity is rooted in childhood disturbance.

Thankfully there have been some studies that explore the role of propaganda in popular culture.

Importantly, the radical movement of is investigated in detail.

Finally, Janet Haines identified the suspect in a line-up.

Alas, it would take some time before such feelings about her divorce would emerge.

As I have already noted, suggested, this lead, inevitably, to disarray.

What is more, ethics can go by the wayside.

In a word, morality can become repugnant.

Look at the following student paragraph before we applied scholarly cosmetic surgery number 2, the magic of introductory phrases.

Utopia or Dystopia – which is our world? The more perfect our world seems, the more imperfect it might be at heart. We have seen a lot of movies lately that depict dystopia of the future. Other movies have shown perfect worlds like Avatar that get ruined by invaders. There also is a way of looking back at history, especially in the United States, both utopian and dystopian. Some people see the past as better, when the white male ruled supreme. Others see the past as dystopic, when slavery, segregation and male dominance were the ways of the world. In real life, it is hard to say which is closer to what we experience on a daily basis. Much of what we do is hard and frustrating, and seems dystopian. But there are things, especially here in Los Angeles when the sun is shining that make life seem perfect some days. It's interesting to explore which one is best to describe our world.

Now look at the same paragraph with some intro words and phrases inserted carefully:

Utopia or Dystopia – which is our world? **Paradoxically,** *the more perfect our world seems, the more imperfect it might be at heart.* **To be sure,** *we have seen a lot of movies lately that depict dystopia of the future.* **On the contrary,** *other movies have shown perfect worlds like Avatar that get ruined by invaders. There also is a way of looking back at history, especially in the United States, both utopian and dystopian. Some people see the past as better, when the white male ruled supreme. Others see the past as dystopic, when slavery, segregation and male dominance were the ways of the world.* **To be clear,** *in real life, it is hard to say which is closer to what we experience on a daily basis. Much of what we do is hard and frustrating, and seems dystopian.* **Still,** *there are things, especially here in Los Angeles when the sun is shining that make life seem perfect some days. It's interesting to explore which one is best to describe our world.*

Five is a lot of intro phrases to pour into one paragraph. But in your introductory paragraph it might be appropriate. For body paragraphs I would reckon you should limit it to three intro phrases. And for the paper as a whole, you wouldn't want to overload these babies onto your pages. Keep a limit of 12 or so.

Now you try:

Use five different intro phrases for the same paragraph above about Utopia.

_____

_____

_____

_____

_____

_____

_____

_____

_____

_____

Your Friends, *Metanoia* and *Correctio.*

Adding phrases like *"if you will,"* and *"that is to say"* or *"per se"* will add a level of meta, self-reflexive rhetoric. These are forms of meta-commentary that are concise ways of indicating to your audience that you are just being approximate, not exact. This is useful in public speaking, of course, where you might not have time to pull the exact term you need right out of your hat. For example, at the Kiwanis banquet as you are bidding farewell to the previous president and accepting the office for yourself, "It gives me great pleasure to succeed, if you will, this great man, the former president."

The "if you will" here gives a quick and clever nod to the audience that you are aware of the potential double entendre of succeed, meaning come after, and succeed, meaning do well.

In writing, although we don't have to come up with words and phrases in an impromptu fashion as public speaker do, it is nevertheless a great addition to a work of scholarly writing to use these types of phrases because even when you have all the time in the world, sometimes there is no word with the precise meaning for the idea you are presenting. For instance, in our previous paragraph about Utopia, we might insert on of these phrases in the following sentence:

*Still, there are things, especially here in Los Angeles when the sun is shining that at times make life Utopian, **if you will**. It's interesting to explore which one is best to describe our world.*

Here, the metanoia "if you will" indicates that you realize it is not Utopia, it just appears to be.

THESE ARE MY FAVORITES:

As it were…. The malignant, as it were, effect of the socialists' argument is that people begin to hate the rich.

So to speak The malignant, so to speak, effect of the socialists' argument is that people begin to hate the…

That is to say. This is a dangerous -- that is to say – malignant effect.

If you will   The malignant, if you will, effect of the socialists' argument is…

Albeit (means it must be admitted, I admit, good to use with em dash)

The malignant – **albeit** *operable—effect of the argument is that people begin to hate the rich.*

Metanoia and correctio can only go after a term that has some ambiguity to it. For instance, you wouldn't say the table, if you will. Unless of course you were out on a picnic and the food was on a boulder that was functioning as a table, if you will. You wouldn't use these terms for solid objects or very clearly defined things, like the Olympics of 2018. There is no Olympics of 2018, as it were. Unless of course, you and your friends were racing down a ski hill in Big Bear engaging in the Olympics of 2018 as it were!

Here are some words that are used in sufficiently ambiguous a manner to warrant the use of metanoia or correctio. Choose which metanoia or correctio you will use for each one and right it in the blank afterwards.

The United States has acted as a suitor, _____, to North Korea, asking China to intercede and make the introductions.

The topic of discussion was chosen, _____, almost by random.

Meditation is a form of prayer, _____, that claims to bring benefits of relaxation to the practitioner.

The process of negotiating Brexit is limping along, _____, without any real clear idea of the end goal.

"That is to say" is the one metanoia and correctio that goes at the beginning of the sentence or clause. It is used to transition from one way of saying something to another perhaps clearer expression of it.

Confederate monuments are being pulled down willy-nilly across the United States; that is to say, there has been little exploration or intelligent discussion about the dangers of applying the standards of the present upon the historical personages of the past.

Here the second part of the sentence clarifies why the speaker called the pulling down of monuments willy nilly – because it hasn't been clearly thought out.

Now you try:

Go through your draft and see if you have some ambiguous words that need clarifying with metanoia or correctio. Try to find at least three.

Chapter Thirteen

WRITING MORE MUSICALLY

If we have succeeded in making our paper a cosmos, a world, then it should be really singing. But are your hills alive with the sound of music? Probably not quite yet. The problem with the music made by most student writing is that it is monotonous. The syntax of almost every student sentence is NOUN – VERB – OBJECT.

Over and over again, this becomes repetitive and sleep inducing. There are some simple things you can do to vary the rhythm of your sentences in your first draft. Again, like the cosmetic techniques introduced in the last chapter, these will become internalized so that you will start to do them in the first draft as well.

USE THE EM DASH

Almost every paragraph of published non-fiction has an em dash in it. Go check for yourself. On the great web site Longform.org you will find the latest long essays published in the United States. Go to the very first one. Scroll down. You will see em dashes – they are slightly longer than the hyphen – used in two ways. One is as a parenthetical aside. Two em dashes on either side of the parenthetical thought work the same way as parentheses to set apart the thought:

A. There are many who believe – quite rightly – that Robert E. Lee was a bigot and a murderer.

This sentence would work fine with parentheses:

B. There are many who believe (quite rightly) that Robert E. Lee was a bigot and a murderer.

Or with no punctuation at all:

C. There are many who believe quite rightly that Robert E. Lee was a bigot and a murderer.

But by far the best is the first one, with the em dashes in example A above. The problem with the parentheses is that they slow down your eye as you read along. The problem with C is that there is no pause as you read, and the author clearly intended you to pause before considering the aside thought – quite rightly. Also, visually, the m-dash provides space in the sentences. In our usual NOUN VERB OBJECT sentence all the letters are clustered together. That is why on longform.org you will find so many m-dashes. They provide a pleasing space to the paragraph and make the task of reading it seem just a little bit easier.

The second way to use the em dash is to set off a tag ending to a sentence.

There are many ways in which the Huguenots did not live up to the rigor of their religion – and sometimes downright betrayed it.

Setting off the last thought this way creates a bit of drama in the sentence. For example, look at the sentence without the em dash. It's perfectly grammatical but it lacks the emphasis on betrayal.

There are many ways in which the Huguenots did not live up to the rigor of their religion and sometimes downright betrayed it.

Now you try:

Find five parenthetical asides or tag endings in your draft and add the em dash. On Windows keyboards you can insert an em dash with the control key plus the hyphen key which is on the number pad, not the hyphen key which is next on the main part of the keyboard. Another way to make the em dash in Word is to type two hyphens from that main part of the keyboard, between the number 0 and the equal sign. Word then changes these two hyphens automatically into the em dash.

WRITE LIKE YODA SPEAKS YOU MUST

Another great way to vary the monotony of the SUBJECT – PREDICATE – OBJECT structure is to write backwards, or to use Yoda-speak, which involves packing information in the front of the sentence before the subject. Rather than "Justine is the most famous of Sade's novels," write: "Most famous of the novels completed by Sade is Justine, which appeared in 1791." This "backwards" structure provides variety to the ordinary student sentence.

Here are few more examples:

FORWARDS: Their readers who seek advice find not inspiration but lecture on the page.

BACKWARDS: Seeking advice, their readers find not inspiration but lecture on the page.

The forwards version of this sentence lacks the drama and emotional hurt of the second version. We set the readers up as people who are seeking advice, only to watch them get hurt in the second part. This way of structuring the sentence not only varies the rhythm, it creates excitement in the language.

WRITING FORWARDS – Women who are ambitious in the workplace and assertive in relationships now seemed – to men – to be completely out of control.

WRITING BACKWARDS – Ambitious in the workplace and rapacious in relationships, women now seemed – to men – to be completely out of control.

This version when written backwards is more cinematic – the women are placed in the foreground in the first shot. Then it seems that the sentence "cuts" to a shot of the men, who think the women are out of control. We must, after all, compete with the cinema and the TV and the internet. The contemporary mind is conditioned to think visually about concepts. In our little double-spaced world of Times New Roman 12-point font, we have to strive to bring a Cinemascope breadth and a Dolby sound weight to our words.

WRITING FORWARDS -- Some doctors who are disillusioned by the apparent inadequacy of introspection instead advocate not talk therapy but anti-depressant medicine to combat anxiety.

WRITING BACKWARDS -- Disillusioned by the apparent inadequacy of introspection, some doctors instead advocate not talk therapy but anti-depressant medicine to combat anxiety.

In the backwards version the doctors become real characters – another thing the movies have that essays don't! The doctors are feeling disillusioned in the first "shot" of the sentence. Then in the next "shot" they go and prescribe medicine. The sentence has a little plot to it, whereas the forwards version is merely a description.

WRITING FORWARDS – Machiavelli was a very busy government employee who was able to concentrate on his writing only when on hiatus from state affairs.

WRITING BACKWARDS – A very busy government employee, Machiavelli was only able to concentrate on his writing only when on hiatus from state affairs.

Again, writing backwards has succeeded in dividing the sentence up into two discrete parts, the unfolding of which plays out like a little movie. In the first part of the movie, Machiavelli is too busy to write. In the second, he finally gets a chance to sit and work on his book.

WRITING FORWARDS – The Italian humans were seeking wisdom and understanding, so they focused on their heritage – Roman civilization.

WRITING BACKWARDS – In seeking wisdom and understanding, the Italian humanists focused on their heritage – Roman civilization.

If you count the number of words in the backwards sentence that come before the subject of the sentence – the Italian humanists – you get a number of five That is good. Usually there are exactly no words before the subject of the sentence. If you can pack a bunch of information in your sentence before you get to the subject, you will have gone a long way in varying the rhythm. Look at the other sentences. They all have at least five words before the subject. Some have more. You should try to stack at least five words before your subject. And you should do this at least once in every paragraph. Then you will have avoided monotony.

WORKING WITH NEGATIVE SPACE

PAINTERS WORK WITH NEGATIVE SPACE – SUPER SCHOLARS DO, TOO. For instance, "It was not until the late 15th Century that the administrative and financial machines of the Western powers reached this point." If the writer had written "In the 15th Century the administrative and financial machines reached this point," he would not have been a super scholar. It is the clever use of the negative that makes things twice as dramatic as they would have been otherwise. Often the narrator of a serious documentary film will employ this strategy, because it just makes everything sound more momentous:

It was not until Albert Einstein arrived on the scene that we would learn just how crazy the universe really is.

That makes Einstein's arrival a really big event, doesn't it? Why are negations so effective? To answer that question, let's first look at why assertions are less effective.

Most student papers are a retinue of assertions: *This is true because this is true. Moreover, this is true. Furthermore, this and that are also true.*

Just as the SUBJECT PREDICATE OBJECT structure becomes monotonous, structuring your language as a series of assertions is also mind-numbing to the reader. Look at this as a possible structure:

This is true (assertion). Moreover, this is true (assertion). But it is not until we realize that this is also true that we really understand the truth. (negation).

In tennis there is the three one rule. Hit three shots crosscourt to the opponent's backhand. Then slam it at the forehand down the line. That's what we will do in the essay as well. For every three assertions, please make one assertion in the form of a negation.

Here are some examples of using negative space:

ASSERTION: In the late 15th century the administrative and financial machines of the Western powers reached this point.

NEGATION: It was not until the late 15th Century that the administrative and financial machines of the Western powers reached this point.

ASSERTION: Other types of TV shows in fact portray men as heroic and capable.

NEGATION: It is not until we examine the other types of tv shows that we realize that men in fact are portrayed as heroic and capable.

ASSERTION: Shows like *Mythbusters* demonstrate the truth about men in TV.

NEGATION: Only when we look at shows like *Mythbuster*s do we find the truth about men in TV

ASSERTION: There is another interesting point to make about men on television.

NEGATION: However, this isn't all there is to say about TV.

ASSERTION: There is another interesting aspect to Mama's portrayal of men in Casa.

NEGATION: But that's not the only interesting aspect of Mama's portrayal of men in Casa.

ASSERTION: When we look at other TV shows that we realize men are sometimes portrayed as intelligent.

NEGATION: Only when we look at other TV shows do we realize men are sometimes portrayed as intelligent.

ASSERTION: Examining the text closely reveals the hidden patriarchy that still lurks in this "women's world".

NEGATION: Only when we examine the text closely do we find the hidden patriarchy that still lurks in this "women's world."

ASSERTION: The Italians offered historical models, the sonnet, or realism in painting and much more.

NEGATION: The Italians had much more to offer than historical models, the sonnet, or realism in painting.

Now you try:

Use the following models to change an assertion into a negation.

A)_____ has much more than _____

EXAMPLE The Italians had much more to offer than historical models, the sonnet, or realism in painting.

ASSERTION: Judith Cofer gives a simplistic analysis of the sexes, but a lot more.

NEGATION:

_____

_____

_____

ASSERTION: Marylin Manson explores the causes of violence other than religion.

NEGATION:

_____

_____

_____

B)_____ has always been _____, but in this case (but now) we see _____(a much more extreme example of) _____

EXAMPLE: Music and song had always played a part in Italian life, both in church and outside. But from the second half of the 15th Century an interest in its potentiality quickened.

ASSERTION: The visual arts were exploding in New York. Andy Wharhol's arrival in the 1950s took it to another level.

NEGATION:

_____

_____

_____

C) There is no sign of _____ going away any time soon.

EXAMPLE: In visual arts Europe saw no hint of Italian faltering.

ASSERTION: In 1930s Europe there was a rising sentiment of nationalism and nativism.

NEGATION:

_____

_____

_____

ARGUMENTATIVE STRUCTURE (tension built into language)

Clauses like, "Although there are many reasons for me to obey you..." are great uses of negative space. You can tell where the author is going, can't you – you just know he's going to be bad. Here we see that language acts like a movie again, by foreshadowing what's to come. The audience loves to guess at what's coming next, and the although clause allows them to do just that. It's an argumentative structure that builds a tension right into language:

1. EXAMPLE: Although it is true that Renaissance Italy was publicly violent and given to grandiloquent displays, the most singular element in the private life of the times may have been moderation.

Although it is true that _____, the most
singular element of _____ is ____.

2. EXAMPLE: While medieval theology was still taken for
   granted, men turned their attention to elaborating a philosophy
   of man.

   While _____ -might be_____, it is also true that
   _____ .

3. EXAMPLE: If anything, Renaissance painting, in spite of its
   realistic appearance, became even more mystical in its message
   than medieval art.

   If anything, _____, in spite of their _____, are even
   more _____ than _____.

4. EXAMPLE: Knowledge and rationality are not necessarily
   subversive; they are, on the contrary, fundamentally related to
   power and must be treated cautiously.

   _____ are not necessarily _____; they are, on the
   contrary, fundamentally _____ and must be treated _____

5. EXAMPLE: Regardless of income or marital status, female
   workers must deal with home and hearth in ways that male
   workers do not.

Regardless of _____, _____ _____ in ways that _____ do not.

Try changing one of your assertions in your first draft into a more argumentative and tense language by using one or more of the above strategies.

THE JOYS OF THE ANTI-CLIMAX

Another great way of varying the rhythm is to use the anti-climax. The anti-climax is a short, sharp little punch that comes, surprisingly, after a long, time-consuming, suspense-filled build-up. It can be a way to knock the wind out of your opponent. It can create a satirical drama – a long list in a crescendo of a sentence, followed by a short anti-climax. The effect is to undercut and undermine the false enthusiasm.

In the 1960s, earnest young people joined other zealous young men and women marching for civil rights, the end of the Viet Nam War, racial justice, no nukes, sexual revolution, equality, free love, and marijuana for everyone. **Then the hippie was born.**

You can see the key to the success of this sentence is the extreme, sudden variation on sentence length – from very, very, long to suddenly quite short.

Now you try:

Try to fill in this anti-climax model sentence with something that makes sense.

Everybody was so excited about _____, bringing us (the joys and thrills of)_____, _____, _____, _____, _____ and _____. Then _____.

Now go to the beginning of your first draft. Think of big long list of things you can build up, only to undermine as you bring out the central dialectic of your paper. It is a good way to establish an original, masterful tone, which is something we'll focus on in the next chapter.

This technique is very useful as an attention grab. Listing in general works well in the beginning of your essay. A list is easier to read, after all, than an ordinary sentence. That is why we write, "Bread, milk, cheese," when we make a shopping list. We don't write, "I should buy bread. I need milk. And maybe I will buy some cheese." Lists give freedom again from the subject and the predicate. They set the reader's mind free. Look at that long section in the series above, where the author lists the things people are marching for. It is easy and fun to read, isn't it? And then, the punch-line. We essay writers can learn from comedians. Build them up and then pull the rug out from under their feet. It's a trick that comics have been using since Vaudeville days.

Example: Doughty, soft, creamy, delightful pastries in the pastry cabinet. Croissants, scones, muffins, cinnamon buns and elephant ears. Drooling, staring, falling deep into the trance, I stare and stare. Then I remember something – I have a vague sense of something but I'm not exactly sure, although it must be admitted in the final analysis I remember it quite clearly. **My New Year's resolution.**

In the above paragraph, the author has a list of adjectives, followed by a list of nouns. Then he tops it off with a list of verbs. But right before the anti-climax it is important to really draw out a long sentence, so the contrast will be apparent. The second to last sentence has four distinct clauses. This is followed by the four-word fragment that is the anti-climax, bolded above.

Now you try

Write three list sentences using different parts of speech. Follow it with a long, complex sentence with at least four clauses. Then top it off with the anti-climax. Your topic: the me-too movement.

LIST 1 – (Maybe a list of the victims)

LIST 2 – (Maybe a list of the crimes)

LIST 3 – (Maybe a list of the accused)

LONG SENTENCE – (maybe something that captures the long, seemingly endless process of revelations that came in the news after first Harvey Weinstein and then others were accused, and the hopes of women everywhere that finally things were going to change, and patriarchy was going to be challenged)

ANTI-CLIMAX – (Something that captures the inevitable backlash – patriarchy reasserts itself)

_____

_____

_____

_____

_____

_____

_____

_____

_____

_____

_____

_____

_____

_____

_____

Chapter Fourteen

A FEW WORDS ON TONE

The tone of most papers professors read is the same –
monotone. I wondered why my students wrote with so little
personality, because I knew from talking to them that they were all
enormously interesting and entertaining personalities. I discovered that
the reason they were suppressing their entertaining personalities in
their papers was the following: respect. They did not want to offend
the teacher. They wanted to be formal and respectful, the way they
were when they were speaking to elders at a family gathering.

Ladies and gentlemen – you are not at a formal gathering. You
are free to be yourself. You can be casual. You can be comic. You
can be zany. You can be anything you want – especially at the
beginning of your paper. Your professor will not be offended. On the
contrary, he will be grateful, because your original or comic tone has
cheered up his stack of dreary papers that he has to correct this
weekend.

The first paragraph is a great place to let your personality loose. I am talking about adding a paragraph to your paper before your introduction where you explored the dialectic and thesis question. This paragraph can be less heady. In the opening paragraph, be entertaining. Hook the interest of your reader. Remember, you are inviting them into a world, a cosmos, a work of art, a heavy metal rock concert, an experience.

VARIOUS ATTENTION GRABS

A good way to grab the reader's attention is to tell a little story, an anecdote that is loosely related to the theme of your paper. Some students list a bunch of little vignettes that are all on the same topic. Sometimes a personal experience is great, or several personal experiences, to set the reader afloat on the river of your thought.

Be cinematic in this opening paragraph. Provide images. Shots. Scenes. All those things you are so familiar with from movies and TV. Use fragments. Like this. Why not? Again, a fragment is easier to read than a complete sentence. Professors will give a free pass to students to be experimental in this first paragraph. You are given poetic license to be just that – poetic. Expressive. Mad.

PUZZLE AND MYSTERY

It's great when you read a first paragraph and you are still not sure what the subject matter of the paper is. In order to find that out, the reader must read on. This, my friends, is the true measure of how successful your attention grab has been – do the readers want to read on?

Now you try:

Imagine you are going to write that essay on marijuana legislation again. But this time, you are going to start with a list of something, a puzzle, a mystery, or some kind of provocation in the attention grabbing first paragraph. You might list the various exotic brands of marijuana that will be available in the upcoming legal pot stores. Or you might list the various methods of ingesting the drug that will be available. You might list the Latin names for the different plants involved. You might list the name of pot stores. The possibilities are endless. You might build to an anti-climax. Or build to a climax – what will happen now the genie is out of the bottle, will we ever be able to put it back in? Use your imagination. Play.

Models for satirical or biting tone:

▶ Use exaggeration or superlatives to undermine a premise in a surprising way.

Women obsessed by social questions can run for Congress now, and nothing is more effective than politics for neutralizing your opinions and toning down your wayward ways.

A. Nowadays there is _____. And nothing is more _____ than _____ for _____.

▶ Question the ordinary definition of a thing by using "so-called" or as in this example, "described as":

Women found an outlet for their energies in jobs, the kind of jobs described as careers, and this made the world safer for the establishment.

▶ Or "previously known as" (to debunk an overly hyped phenomenon.)

There's space, of course, previously known as the sky, called the last adventure.

▶ Or just use "fingernail quotes":

"Frontier" now refers to freeze-dried or virtual adventure travel.

B. The so-called (or self-described) _____ is (are) really just _____ in disguise.

C. Everybody was so excited about _____, bringing us (the joys and thrills of)_____, _____, _____, _____, _____ and _____. Then _____.

▶ Don't forget to concede the opposition some point – it shows that you're objective. But then undercut that concession as quickly as you can:

> *Certainly, women are better off now, at least in civilized countries, with all our fine new opportunities to behave ourselves and follow the rules. Still it's nice to know there were Amazons out there, once upon a time.*

D. Of course, it's true that _____, which is so wonderful because of _____ and _____. Still, it's nice to know that _____.

YOU SHOULD NOT SAY SHOULD

I have observed over the years that students, eschewing the hard, creative work of cosmological writing, tend to default about half-way through their argument into a ranting tone that uses the word "should" incessantly. Telling us what "should" be fixed in society is problematic – and is certainly not an argument. Tonally, too, it is off-putting. Ask yourself, do like being told what you should be doing?

The other day I was driving with my older sister when she announced, "You should come to a complete stop, you know." In fact, my car was completely at rest in a complete stop when she said it. It was rather infuriating to be told what I should do when I was already doing it – but I guess that is what older sisters are for. I tried to be a duck, and let it bounce off like water off my back. But a little while later she was at it again, telling me I should get my car looked at because it was making a noise. OK, fair enough, I let it wash off my back again. But finally, she said, "You should slow down!" and I lost it, because I was going five miles per hour under the speed limit.

"Enough with the criticisms!" I snapped. "Geez!"

Telling people what they should be doing is a sure way to 1) be ignored, as I was trying to ignore my sister, or worse, 2) get your head bitten off. Sorry I snapped at you, sister!

Anyhow, despite all my instruction about how to break down the dialectic, analyze the terms, and create a meaningful philosophical question, about three quarters of the way through their papers, my students still sometimes lapse into, "We should stop polluting the planet," or "We shouldn't discriminate against people," or "Society should accept people for what they are."

I discourage my students from using the term "society" when they actually mean "people." But a worse sin is the "should." It turns your wonderful world – your cosmos – your world of idea and analysis and distinction into – well, it turns it into a toothache.

"You should go to the dentist," every toothache says. And of course, we resist, hoping that the toothache will go away. But there it is again the next day, saying, "I'm still hurting you, you should definitely go to the dentist and have this looked at."

Alright! I'll go to the dentist. But I don't need my students telling me what else should happen.

The other objection I have about "should" is that musically and rhythmically and tonally it is not tuneful. It is dissonant and painful to listen to, like a rant. It is likely that you've heard a few rants in your day, critical rants. Maybe a parent or even a friend went on a five-minute soliloquy ranting about what you have been doing wrong and how ungrateful you are and how...At this point you probably stopped listening, so you don't know what else you are besides ungrateful.

YOU SHOULD DO THIS INSTEAD OF SHOULD

Instead of "should," if you must make a claim about how to improve things at some point in your paper, I suggest modesty and whimsy.

MODESTY – this is achieved through qualifying statements that lessen the certainty and righteousness of your "should." Phrases that qualify your suggestions are: maybe, perhaps, or might.

"Maybe we should do something about saving those whales."

"Perhaps this evidence will convince us to take steps to reduce carbon emissions."

"It might be time to get rid of these Confederate statues once and for all."

These three statements above are saying "should" but in a nicer way that sounds easier on the ear. You are not claiming to "know better" than anyone else what must happen. You are just making modest suggestions.

WHIMSY

Whimsy is achieved through replacing the should with a whimsical, dreamy possibility.

"Wouldn't it be great if no more dolphins got trapped in plastic bags that pollute their ocean home?"

"In a perfect world, we wouldn't have to deal with micro aggressions or verbal slights in the work place or at school."

"How wonderful it would be for a woman to be able to walk down any city street without being catcalled."

The tone of these whimsical wishes is exactly that – wishful, hopeful, optimistic. The music of these sentences is not the least bit off-putting. And finally, these sentences do not seem impulsive or immature. They seem well thought out and adult. That's what we want to shoot for in our essays. Wouldn't it be great if we could achieve that?

(See what I did there?)

Now you try:

Turn these should into more palatable statements by using either modesty or whimsy.

1. We should stop ruining the earth.

_____

_____

2. Society should stop judging people based on their skin color

_____

_____

3. We should have more equality.

_____

_____

4. America should be kinder to refugees.

_____

_____

5. The president should not be so disrespectful.

_____

_____

6. The people who run Wall Street should be punished.

_____

_____

7. The media should stop trying to cause all these problems.

_____

_____

Now look for anything in your paper that approaches "should." In the next draft, either cut it out or use the techniques you just learned to make it sound more musical.

Chapter Fifteen

LEARN TO SPEAK A FOREIGN LANGUAGE IN FIVE MINUTES!

Using *vis-à-vis* properly can elevate the tone of your inquiry as only a French phrase can. How about throwing in *ersatz*? Did you know that the term *ersatz* means sawdust, and it came from prisoners of war in Germany who were served bread made from sawdust instead of flour? Latin phrases are also extremely popular in academic writing. A good use of a Latin phrase can be the *sine qua non* of a good scholarly paper. In this section we seriously examine how to avoid seeming overly pompous when using foreign words and how to avoid using them incorrectly. In your second draft, you can use these phrases to color your creation--your world of ideas--with a little bit of extra weight.

Scholars love Latin. The first universities were founded by the Catholic Church in the middle ages, and the courses were taught in Latin. Latin, then, is the first language of scholarship. Although it is no longer taught regularly in the United States, Latin nevertheless appears with regularity in scholarly articles.

LATIN

I give the definition below for these most common Latin phrases used by scholars.

qua

Advertising **qua** art can be judged by aesthetic criteria only._

(as)

Why use *qua* instead of the word as? More than as, it also carries the meaning that the one thing is considered to be of the same class or category as the other. This is not implied by the English term. For example, if we said advertising as art, it would lead to confusion – are we talking about art used in advertising?

per se

At the same time, we must not forget that essentialism and universalism are not opposites ***per se***

(exactly)

This functions as a correctio, like as it were or if you will, and always comes after the noun, not before. Not "per se opposites."

a priori

The state, for anarchists, is *a priori* oppression, no matter what form it takes.

(as a fundamental assumption true from the beginning, a given)

This is useful because creating a cosmological piece of writing means working with some fundamental a priori assumptions about the world – always.

mirabile dictu

And then, *mirabile dictu*, between the piers, leaping from wave to wave as it rushed at headlong speed, swept the strange schooner before the blast, with all sail set, and gained the safety of the harbor.

(marvelous to recount)

This is useful for satirical or sardonic tone because, after all, things rarely live up the hype – the Latin can emphasize this.

ad infinitum -

The author makes claim after claim ***ad infinitum*** that are not borne out by the facts.

(to infinity without end)

ad nauseum

The first article repeats its claims ***ad nauseum*** that Pollack was a genius but that does not make them any more legitimate.

(to the point of disgust)

Nobody wants to use the word vomit or throw up in a paper. This is a sophisticated and respectable way to do it.

sine qua non

The perfect cake is the ***sine qua non*** of the carefully planned modern wedding...

(essential part of the whole)

We already know *qua*. See how quickly we're learning this language! This is useful because our trajectory in the essay is toward a central principle. The *sine qua non*!

status quo:

The right wants to maintain the **status quo,** which in this case would mean silencing the students and their demand for change.

(the current state of things)

This term is used today to designate the existing state or condition of things or the powers that be. A thing that essayists often challenge.

FRENCH

Par excellence

Stirner reveals himself as an anti-authoritarian thinker ***par excellence.***

(the best of its kind)

We aim for the *par excellence* in our cosmos, in so many ways. We want our world of distinctions and ideas and argument to be an essay *par excellence.*

vis-à-vis

Let's look at the GDP *vis-à-vis* production

(in relation to, literally means face to face with)

Looking at an issue or a question vis-à-vis a text is what we worked on in the chapter 4-6 of this book – only we didn't speak French then. Now we do

Chapter Sixteen

ACADEMIC JARGON JAMBOREE

Every field has its own jargon. If this were a book on aerospace, you would expect to find a glossary of some of the terms and specialized language of the field of aerospace. The field of academic writing in the humanities is no different. It has its own specialized language, one that sometimes takes ten years in a PhD program to master. However, there is no reason for you to eschew that jargon as a beginning academic writer. After all, they let beginning painters use paint, don't' they? They don't wait until the painter has been accepted into a Master's program. (Notice I have been using the word "eschew". That is a good piece of academic jargon. It means to avoid.) What words like "eschew" do to your cosmos is give it that badge of honor or credential that a paper needs. It lets the reader knows that you are officially in the world of scholarship, and that's why you are using a bit of jargon of scholarship. Don't worry, you won't lose your own authentic voice by throwing in some jargon. You will always be you, and nobody will write exactly like you, because you have been writing from your most creative self. Even the way you use the jargon will be unique to you. So let's proceed.

DISCOURSE

I have identified some core pieces of academic jargon that are currently in vogue in academia. The number one hit— discourse. Everything is *discourse*. Your gender is discourse. It is determined by the way your culture speaks about male or female. Your house is discourse. It's a discussion that takes place between building materials and empty space.

Can you find a place in your second draft where you can use the word discourse? Anywhere that interpretation is going on of any kind is a good place for discourse. For example, in the following sentence, which word could be changed to discourse:

Advertising makes women want to be a certain way.

The way to understand the academic use of the word discourse is that it is the power above all other powers. It is the absolute monarch, in charge of all things. If we were in this absolute monarch's kingdom, for instance, it wouldn't be advertising that makes women want to be a certain way, it would be the King, because the King is in charge of all things. Thus, substituting the word discourse for King, we arrive at:

*The **discourse** of gender identity found in advertising makes women want to be a certain way.*

ESSENTIALIST

Students get confused because essential means important. But essentialist means something else altogether, and it's a very important academic concept right now. The essentialist position is one that academics, in fact, eschew. It is the base position. It is the wrong position. It believes that things have identity in and of themselves, innately. But we academics know that NOTHING IS GOOD OR BAD, as said Shakespeare, but our thinking that makes is so. Our discourse **constructs** this identity.

*Conservatives take an **essentialist** position on crime, believing that criminals are essentially and innately evil.*

CONSTRUCTED

Students get confused again, because this doesn't mean construct in the sense of a construction site with bulldozers etc. It means constructed out of culture and language.

*My identity as a unicorn was not **constructed** by my parents – it's something I chose by myself.*

LIMINAL

The most exciting events that take place are **liminal**. That is, they take place in the borderline, the no-man's land between two places.

*The poem describes **liminal** moments between waking and sleep.*

INTERSECTION

This liminal place is called an **intersection**.

*The immigrant forms a self at the **intersection** of two cultures, neither of which he fully belongs to any more.*

SIGNIFIER

Red means stop and green means go, right? Have you seen any good **signifiers** lately?

*The author points out how the everyday world of the impoverished contains **signifiers** of lack and absence.*

POSIT

To define something as so: I **posit** academic writing, in this book, as a creative act akin to creation of the cosmos itself.

*Jones **posits** fairytales as philosophical explorations, not just bedtime stories.*

COLLOQUY

This is a meeting or a conversation. In fact, all academic papers are colloquies between the author and the reader. They meet in the world of the paper. It's not a bad thing to call a spade a spade, so go ahead and at some point, become self-conscious and call your paper a colloquy on whatever subject you're discoursing on.

*Thus, ends our **colloquy** on academic jargon.*

PSEUDO-, QUASI-, FAUX, ERSATZ

These are four hand grenades you can throw at your opponents during the video game battle royal that is your academic paper. They each mean that your opponent is a phony. There is nothing worse than being revealed as a fraud, is there? That's what these words do. Whoever challenges your thesis must be guilty of one of these. How to choose which grenade to lob? They are all subtly different.

Pseudo is a prefix that means fake, for instance, pseudoscientific. It means that the person sounds like they're being scientific, but they really aren't.

This is a **pseudointellectual** *approach to the problem that only seems intelligent but is quite foolish.*

Quasi means almost. Think of a quasar, it is almost a star but not quite, according to the scientists who first detected their radio signals. But they were just pseudoscientists. Now we know quasars are actually stars. Never mind, you can use this term to say that your opponent is almost an intellectual but not quite.

The **quasi-***Brechtian theatre of the production reminds the audience that they are witnessing a contrived performance, not a reality.*

Faux. Whatever you do, don't say "My opponent is faux." Faux like the other words in this group is the adjective that must come before the noun. You know faux fur? It's made of synthetic material, but it looks exactly like fur. Similarly, your opponent's idea looks exactly like a valid point but in fact it's a faux argument.

The **faux** *urbanism of this design is actually quite dated.*

Ersatz. This is the sawdust inside the bread. It is completely unsatisfying in its imitation. If you call your opponent on his/her ersatz reasoning, you will destroy him/her.

The **ersatz** *logic of this line of reasoning can only lead us to absurd conclusions.*

Now you try:

Go through your paper and see where you can fit in this vocabulary, if at all. It might not be the right time and the place for any of this jargon. Please don't use it unless it really fits.

Chapter Seventeen

OUR REVELS NOW ARE ENDED

And here we have come to the end of the world. The cosmos of this writing manual is reaching its conclusion. I hope your second draft has turned out to be an even more wonderful world of distinctions than your first, and that all your drafts in the future will be even more cosmologically grand.

Before you leave, I would like to thank you for going on this journey with me. We've dared to take a radically different approach to academic writing. What we've done, really, is to make academic writing more like creative writing. The three adjectives I would like you to carry forward with you as you continue working on your essay writing skills are: God-like, artistic and heavy metal.

You are not God, but you can adopt the creative energy of a world-creating deity when you write – anything. Please don't forget that you have this strange generative ability as a conscious intelligence.

You are an artist, though. That's why I hope you paint and sculpt your future work like a true artist, in an artist's studio, metaphorically, when you sit down at your desk. Paint with your ideas. Make a movie with your reasoning. Play a symphony with those words.

Finally, go at it with a heavy metal attitude of extreme energy. When the great soccer coach Jurgen Klopp came to the Liverpool soccer team, he invented the term "heavy metal football." You could see it in the way the Liverpool players started approaching the game. They were on a tear. They were blasting through the opponent's defenses. They were supremely entertaining to watch.

You should aim to be supremely energetic and entertaining with your argument. Don't slip into the somnolent, dirge-like tone of the student. Remain yourself – vibrant and original. Heavy metal.

Maybe there is another style of music or art or fashion that conveys the sense of jubilant creativity that I am calling for. Write it here. Make a solemn vow that you will never again write perfunctory essays.

I, _____(your name)_____, solemnly swear to always be _____(your heavy metal adjective)_____ in my writing and in my life.

For more resources on writing, please go the web site, Cracktheessay.com. You will find loads more scholarly vocabulary and tricks of the trade that will help enhance your writing. Thank you once again.

APPENDIX

INTERTEXTUALITY/RE-READING

1. The (one text) suggests a way of reading (the other text) that questions, identifies, interrogates, undermines, enriches, brings out, highlights, emphasizes, destabilizes, complicates, simplifies, examines….._____.

2. The (first text) suggests a different way

3. of reading the (second text), not as a _____, but as a _____. There are two aspects of the (second text) that I would like to examine in order to clarify what I mean by this way of reading the text.

4. Looked at through the lens of (the second text), the _____in the first text becomes immediately apparent.

B. FOR CORRESPONDENCE

1. Another facet of (the first text) which chimes with the ____ (in the second text) is _____.

2. The first text here sheds an instructive light on ____ (something in the second text)

3. The author of (the first text) offers an illuminating perspective on (something in the second text.)

4. (Something in the first text) underscores the importance of (something in the second text).

5. The second text repeats the central themes of, parallels, corresponds with, correlates with, reworks, refashions, reshapes, resembles, extends, recalls (the first text).

C. FOR DIFFERENCE

1. (Something in the first text) undermines (an idea presented in the second text) by emphasizing _____.
2. The (newer text) refuses to, fails to, denies, resists, does not perform _____ which its antecedent, (the first text) demands, celebrates, claims, posits etc.
3. What becomes clear from close-reading of both texts is how (one text is more complex, more interesting, more nuanced, more sophisticated, more intelligent, more modern, more engaging, more accurate than the other text). The _____ in (the first text) is striking, (clear, undeniable, ever-present, highlighted) whereas in the (second text) _____(some difference)
4. Particularly significant is the fact that (in the first text) _____. In comparison, in the second text (some difference)_____.
5. In effect, the second text provides more, greater, stronger, richer_____.
6. The _____that is granted in the first text is withheld in the second.
7. …gives a different perspective on…..

D. DEVELOPMENT

As your analysis moves along, each new element both builds on and departs from the previous ones.

8. This **text** both builds on and **departs from the** simple promise of its title,

9. _____ both builds on and departs from the idea of _____.

10. The second text extends the notion of _____ to_____

11. ....reiterates this notion of _____ in the story of _____.

12. …. Develops, rewrites, reinvests, reworks, reconsiders,

13. What is important to remember, however, is that in the second text _____ whereas in the first text _____. Both authors had distinct _____and were influenced by distinct _____.

14. This text puts a different gloss on that text which emphasizes _____ rather than _____.

15. _Example:_ Adele de Senange is an interesting variation on the theme: the sweetness of the couple and of the young man who loves ...

_____ can be read as an interesting variation on the theme of _____.

About the author

Simon Black has been teaching writing at the university level since 2001. Previously, he wrote novels, plays, films, TV. Scripts, blogs, songs and articles for magazines and academic journals. He brings to the practice of analytic and argumentative writing a distinctive approach that stems from the various fields of creative writing that he has practiced. He learned academic writing at his alma mater, Columbia College, and owes a deep debt of gratitude to his Professor of Comparative Literature, the late Karl Ludwig Selig. He lives in Los Angeles with his wife and children and their dog, Mac.

Made in United States
North Haven, CT
18 June 2024